OUTDOOR CLASSICS

Secrets of
SUCCESSFUL TURKEY HUNTING

Publishing
P/S
Solutions

OUTDOOR CLASSICS

Secrets of
SUCCESSFUL TURKEY HUNTING

Publishing Solutions, LLC
Chaska, Minnesota

OUTDOOR CLASSICS
Secrets of SUCCESSFUL TURKEY HUNTING

ISBN 1-932533-01-X (hardcover)
ISBN 1-932533-02-8 (tradepaper)

Publishing Solutions, LLC
1107 Hazeltine Blvd., Suite 470
Chaska, MN 55318
James L. Knapp, President
www.ipubsolutions.com

Printed in the USA.

Contents

About OUTDOOR CLASSICS

The OUTDOOR CLASSICS series from Publishing Solutions, LLC, brings to you the very best in outdoor writing over the last 15 years. Rather than let the passage of time allow these terrific books to be lost to a new generation of outdoor enthusiasts, this series re-introduces some of the best advice available on the selected hunting and fishing topics.

The information in this series has been time-tested and field proven. It has been written by professionals in their field who share with you the wisdom of their success.

Equipment will change. However, the basics of the outdoor enthusiast's quest for game and fish remain constant. If you want to know the basics for success, this series is for you.

This book was originally published as *Turkey Hunting Tactics*. Thank you to the staff at North American Affinity Clubs for their help in bringing this series back to life. The publisher especially wishes to thank Nancy Evensen, Tom Carpenter, Heather Koshiol and Julie Cisler for their hard work and contributions.

Photo Credits

Photos in this book were provided by the author. In addition to examples of his own talent, he has included photos from Sara Bright, Bill Miller, Russ Reason, Dr. Dan Speake and Tim Tucker.

About The Author

John Phillips is recognized as one of North America's leading authorities on turkey hunting, because, as John says, "I've learned just about everything that *doesn't* work to take a gobbler. I've made the mistakes that hunters make when turkey hunting, and I've learned from those mistakes."

Phillips credits the turkey hunters he's known and the life he's led for most of his turkey hunting knowledge and skill. His love for the outdoors was nurtured by his hunting and fishing family—particularly by John's father, W.A., Sr., whose time afield with his family came first, and by John's older brother, Archie, who allowed John to tag along in the woods with him almost as soon as John could walk. Today both brothers are professional outdoorsmen.

John's turkey hunting education began in college in the mid-1960s at Livingston University in Southwest Alabama. The university is located in the heart and soul of southern turkey hunting country. Many of the counties Phillips hunted had never known a closed season for turkey. It was rumored that some of Phillips' college buddies who helped him learn how to turkey hunt could call gobblers before they could say "Daddy."

Not only did Phillips' fascination with hunting elusive gobblers begin in college but also his desire to become a writer. As Phillips remembers, "A friend in law school had an article published in

Outdoor Life. After reading that article, I believed that if he could write and sell an outdoor story to a major magazine like that, I could too. I knew I didn't have the background or training to be a writer, since I was a physical education major with a history minor. However, I'd always enjoyed hearing and reading stories about the outdoors. And my dad was a spellbinding storyteller.''

After service obligations and running YMCAs for several years, Phillips made a decision that would change his life forever.

''I decided that being an outdoor writer couldn't be any more difficult than becoming a carpenter and learning how to build a house. I felt that I would have to serve a five year apprenticeship to learn my craft and that there would be hurt, discouragement and disaster along the way to my goal. Just like most carpenters learn to drive a nail straight by smashing their thumbs two or three times and falling off a ladder, I figured that my course in becoming a writer would follow a similar pattern.''

And sure enough, Phillips wrote and sent off 48 magazine manuscripts before the first article ever sold. During that time he was also writing a weekly outdoor column for several newspapers in Alabama and producing a daily, syndicated outdoor radio show for 28 stations. That was back in 1973.

Phillips paid his dues as a writer. Since that time, his work has been published by such magazines as *North American Hunter*, *Outdoor Life*, *Sports Afield*, *Bassin'*, *Fishing Facts*, *Mother Earth News* and *Progressive Farmer*. His work has also appeared in Game and Fish Publications, Harris Publications and Aqua-Field Publications. He serves as the editor-at-large for *The Complete Sportsman* and senior editor for *Crappie World Magazine*.

Turkey Hunting Tactics is Phillips' sixth book. His other books include *Outdoor Life's Complete Turkey Hunting, Bass Fishing With The Skeeter Pros, How To Make More Profit In Taxidermy* and *Deer & Fixings Cookbook*.

Phillips feels that his greatest assets to his writing career have been his wife, Denise, who not only serves as mother to children Kate, John and Hunter, but also housekeeper, editor, business manager and best friend; his mother-in-law, Marjolyn McLellan, who has been his secretary, receptionist and tireless source of encouragement over many years; and his editors, who have helped mold and shape not only his work but also his talent.

If Phillips has any talent for turkey hunting, he believes it comes from hard work. ''Any skill is more the result of hard work, failure and learning from your mistakes than anything else.''

In 1988 Phillips hunted for 49 consecutive days for turkey in three states. He harvested Easterns, Merriams and Rio Grande gobblers. But Phillips' goal in turkey hunting is not strictly the bagging of the bird.

"If I call up a turkey and could have killed him but choose not to, or if I call up a tom that someone else takes, then I'm just as satisfied, and often more satisfied, than if I squeeze the trigger. The real sport of hunting turkey for me is to outsmart the gobbler and get him close enough to be taken. What happens from that point on doesn't really matter to me.

"I enjoy seeing another sportsman get excited, nervous and anxious as a gobbler starts to walk in to where we are, and then watching that hunter gain control of his emotions, settle down into a shooting position and harvest his first tom. Those memories last longer and mean more to me than the ones of the turkey I hunt myself. The excitement of the hunt—more than the taking of the tom—is what calls me into the woods each spring when the trees begin to bud and the gobblers sing their love calls."

Dedication

All that a man is and all that he has attained can only be seen in what he leaves behind. The future he makes for others is far more important than the now he creates for himself. And my family's future in the beloved sport of turkey hunting will rest in the hands of the ones to whom I dedicate this book: Katherine Elizabeth Phillips, John Edward Phillips, Jr., and William Hunter Phillips. They are the greatest trophies the Good Lord could ever give.

Introduction:
The Agony And The Ecstasy

There was once a gobbler, the Mad Baron of Piney Wood Knoll, that captured the minds of most of the male population of an entire southern community. Every man and boy in the town felt that harvesting this legendary tom was his holy calling.

Old timers recall that some of the town's husbands and wives were on the verge of divorce because this gobbler demanded more time of the men than the ladies received. Businesses, they say, were about to close because the Mad Baron kept the menfolk of the community away from their work until noon each day of the turkey season. And the young people? They couldn't court each other because the young men spent every waking hour planning, plotting and conniving a scheme to take the Mad Baron.

Ambushes were laid, and assassination plots were planned.

There was even one attempt to set fire to the woods and drive the Mad Baron out to the hunters. Snares were placed along game trails; trail timers were used to plot the course of the gobbler.

The battle between this community—which shall remain nameless—and the Mad Baron was not simply a one-spring skirmish. The war raged for three years, resulting, some say, in seven divorces and 22 lost jobs. Realizing that there was little hope for the community unless the Mad Baron was removed, one wiry young man, sound of both body and mind, concocted the plan that lead to the Baron's eventual demise.

"As the Mad Baron's toenails touched the soft earth beneath his tree I squeezed the trigger of the 10 gauge, and the big cannon reported."

"Well, I figured I either had to kill the baron or stand by and watch my friends and hometown suffer," said Sage Thomas (name changed to protect the hero). "So I went to a friend in a nearby community who had a 10 gauge. I borrowed that shotgun and three shells.

"Then I waited until the worst morning of the spring, when the rain was pouring down, the sky was lit with lightning and the thunder was rolling in. I went to the knoll where the Mad Baron began his gobbling.

"Every time the thunder clashed, that turkey shock gobbled. Through the mud and rain, I belly crawled to a small bush about 50 yards from where he was roosting. Under the cover of darkness, I hid in ambush and waited for that aggravating bird to fly down at first light.

"Each lightning flash silhouetted the Mad Baron in his giant water oak. He was a terrible renegade, but I couldn't shoot him off that limb. I couldn't live with the disgrace of taking the Mad Baron like that. So I waited in the pouring rain.

"When the white string of morning light was slowly pulled across the black covers of darkness, that big tom ruffled his feathers, lifted his head, stretched his wings and pitched off the limb. As the Mad Baron's toenails touched the soft earth beneath his tree I squeezed the trigger of the 10 gauge, and the big cannon reported.

"I returned to town and showed the Mad Baron to everyone, not to prove my prowess as a hunter, but rather to show the townsfolk that the villain was dead and that we could return to our everyday affairs of life."

The gobble of a wild turkey, like the Mad Baron's, has a mystical, addictive power. The sound is as powerful as the wailing of the sirens whose seductive songs caused the ancients to sail their ships into disaster. The only remedy to counteract the lure of the sirens' melodies was discovered by the Greeks; they stuffed their ears with cotton. Likewise, ear stuffing may be the only way to keep a hunter from being lured to the madness caused by a wild turkey's gobble.

Have you ever known a man who was in love with a beautiful woman to the point that she dominated his mind and spirit? All he thought about was that woman, but she didn't return his affection. That happens to a turkey hunter when he hunts a wily gobbler that won't come to his calling. Some men can't eat, sleep or think of anything but the gobbler they're chasing.

Sometimes, a simple introduction to the sport is all that's required. Take for example the author's now teenage son, John.

After permitting him to hunt with a friend when he was 11 years old, John was infected with turkey fever. This past year, when asked to hunt with his father on opening morning, he replied, "Well, Dad, I would, but I promised one of the other men in our hunting club that I would guide and call for him."

One obvious symptom of turkey fever is an inflated ego. It usually emerges after the hunter has taken his first turkey. However, after two or three birds thoroughly humiliate the hunter, his ego deflates to its proper size.

For some people there's no hunter more accomplished than the turkey hunter. He combines all hunting and woodsmanship skills to take his quarry. For turkey hunters, the sport is the ultimate chess game for the nimrod. All other hunting sports are merely contests of checkers.

If you've played chess, you know that when you make a move, you not only have to determine how that move will work to your advantage but how that move can disadvantage your opponent. But while deciding what to do next, you must also determine what to do if your opponent counters your move with one of about 20 options. A chess player makes his moves not only to win but also to keep from losing.

The game of hunting turkey is much the same. For every move the hunter makes, the turkey can choose from 20 countermoves. Therefore if the hunter only knows strategies that will help him win, but hasn't worked out tactics that will prevent him from losing, he will be defeated.

Let's look at the winning techniques and countermoves for today's turkey hunter.

1

The Wild Turkey

The wild turkey is native exclusively to North America. With seven to 10 million roaming this continent in the early days, the turkey were easy targets. Indian children often would be assigned the task of taking the birds. Many Indian tribes called the tom Old Chief Galagina or The Gobbling One.

The wild turkey is a member of the order Galliforme, which includes grouse, prairie chicken, ptarmigan, quail, pheasant, peafowl and guineafowl. The wild turkey has many of the characteristics of other species in the order, including a down-curved bill, large, heavy feet with three toes in front and a shorter one behind. They are also good runners and can fly well for short distances. Typically, a turkey can fly at 38-42 miles per hour. One turkey was detected by a special radar device doing 55 miles per hour. Turkey, however, can not swim. Like the peacock, wild turkey have iridescent feathers and a gentleman-like strut.

At the first Thanksgiving celebration in 1621 Indians donated "great stores of wild Turkies" as their share of the feast. Settlers and frontiersmen not only killed the turkey for food but also used the turkey's many useful parts to make their lives easier. The result was a substantial decline in the turkey population.

By 1813, turkey had disappeared from Connecticut. Increasing habitat loss as well as the encroachment of civilization caused a

Back in the early days, frontiersmen took the birds with flintlocks and black powder. At one time, North America supported seven to 10 million turkey.

further decline in the nation's turkey flocks so that by 1851 no turkey were left in Massachusetts.

After the Civil War, in the 1860s until the early 20th Century, market hunting for turkey was at its height. One exporting firm in St. Louis filled a London order for 700 dozen wild turkey. The year was 1881. By the late 1800s, turkey were gone from much of their original 39 state range, even in the Midwest.

Then in the early 20th century, President Theodore Roosevelt asked Congress to set aside areas for wildlife refuges and to start using science as a way to help America's dwindling wildlife. From that time until the 1930s, private game preserves were established, with sportsmen setting up laws to protect and manage the animals.

In 1935 the Cooperative Wildlife Research Unit Program was established. The Federal Aid in Wildlife Restoration Act—more commonly known as the Pittman-Robertson Act—was passed in 1937. This Act directly aided the failing American turkey flocks by training wildlife professionals and helping states hire these managers.

Alabama, Virginia, Louisiana, Texas and Missouri were the first states with wild turkey research programs. These research programs located the existing populations of turkey, provided information for hunting seasons and selected areas for restocking programs. These programs were vital to the survival of wild turkey, because by the end of World War II, only 30,000 remained in the U.S. Many of those early projects didn't succeed, because game farm turkey were used. The birds were not self-sufficient and had lost the wariness they needed to survive. The game farm turkey also introduced poultry diseases—unheard of at that time—to the wild flocks. That decimated the wild turkey population.

However, turkey in the West had not been overhunted, and cars, people, animals and buildings were not as intensive per acre as in the East. In the '40s and early '50s some western turkey flocks actually increased. For instance, 15 wild turkey trapped in New Mexico in 1935 increased to a 1,000-bird flock by 1958.

Numerous factors improved other turkey numbers. When the cannon-projected net trap, originally used for taking waterfowl, was used for transplanting wild turkey, these wild birds lived and reproduced in their new homes. Improved forest management, better law enforcement and an increasing concern for conservation also aided the growth of the wild turkey populations. Biologists even transplanted turkey into habitats beyond their ancestral range.

The National Wild Turkey Federation (NWTF) was incorpo-

Through the restocking efforts of hunters and state conservation departments, wild turkey populations have continued to grow.

rated as a nonprofit conservation and education organization in 1973. In turn, they established the NWTF Research Foundation in 1981 to solicit funds from private and corporate sources and to administer these funds for wild turkey research nationwide. In 1986 the NWTF signed an agreement with the U.S. Forest Service to provide money and volunteers to maintain and improve wild turkey habitat and conduct research on Forest System lands.

Even with a national flock of more than 2.5 million turkey in 1988—and populations in every state except Alaska—NWTF biologists continue to improve flocks. In 1987, only 100 eastern wild turkey lived on 12 million acres of suitable habitat in East Texas. So in 1988 the NWTF teamed up with the Texas Parks and Wildife Department to work with several southeastern states and Iowa to restock eastern turkey in the region.

Part of the reason for the success of turkey populations lies in the uniqueness and self-sufficiency of the wild turkey. Biologists say that the turkey's ability to use more than 354 species of plants and 313 kinds of small animals enable these wild birds to feed on a wide variety of plant and animal life.

When food is available, a turkey can eat up to a pound of food per meal thanks to a powerful gizzard that can crush the hardest foods. Even in the snow, turkey can scratch as deep as a foot to find food.

Nature also has ensured that each turkey poult is strong, able to resist disease and grow. Usually only the dominant gobbler in each area breeds the females. That means that a great number of eggs will be laid with few of those infertile. Gobblers prepare for mating season weeks before it begins by feeding heavily. Soon the turkey's chest is bulging and forms a breast sponge, a mass of thick, cellular tissue that the tom lives on during mating season. Then the gobbler doesn't have to worry about eating. Instead he can concentrate on mating, and wait until after the season to feed and replenish his strength.

An interesting sidenote to the toughness of turkey: If a hen's eggs or nest are destroyed, and she mates with a bird other than the dominant gobbler, a large proportion of the eggs will be infertile.

The ability of the turkey's feathers to insulate and conserve heat helps a turkey face bad weather. The down feathers are those closest to the bird's body. These down feathers are covered by vein feathers, which are contour feathers that shield the down and give the turkey a sleek look. Turkey face into strong winds to prevent the wind from getting underneath the contour feathers.

The wild turkey, a magnificent creation with acute survival instincts, has been as much a part of American history as the men who wrote it.

2

Turkey Hunting
Across North America

The wild turkey, *Meleagris gallopava*, is hunted in 47 states, Mexico and Ontario. The species consists of six subspecies with differences mainly in weight, coloration and habitat.

Ocellated Turkey. The Ocellated turkey is the ancestor of our domesticated turkey. These birds were hunted extensively in Central America before being shipped by the early conquistadors back to Europe to be domesticated.

Eastern Turkey. The eastern wild turkey has been successfully restocked in more than 30 states. According to the National Wild Turkey Federation, this most sought-after species holds the record for the heaviest turkey—at 33¼-pounds—and the best atypical turkey—with seven beards and 183.75 points.

Rio Grande Turkey. Rio Grande gobblers are found throughout the arid Southwest. Texas, Oklahoma and California typically yield the largest birds.

Merriam Turkey. Merriam turkey are taken from a wide range of territory including South Dakota, California, Washington, Colorado, Minnesota, New Mexico, Nebraska and Wyoming. Its tail feathers are much whiter than any other subspecies of turkey.

Gould Turkey. The Gould turkey resembles the Merriam gobbler in that the tips of its tail feathers are also white, but not as intense. Found predominantly in Mexico, the Gould is slightly smaller than the Merriam.

Oceola Turkey. The Oceola turkey is found predominantly in Florida. For this reason it is sometimes called the Florida turkey. Although this bird resembles the Eastern turkey in coloration, its body size is smaller.

Turkey hunting, anywhere in North America, requires skills which are not needed in many of the other hunting sports. A turkey hunter must...

... be swift of foot, since he may have to run a large circle to get in front of a turkey that gobbles and then walks away from him.

... be able to endure pain, because wading a cold creek, climbing a high mountain, sliding down a gravel bank or belly crawling through a half acre of low briars may be required to get into position.

... have the patience of Job to sit for two to five hours without moving, which may be the only possible tactic to bag a wise old gobbler.

... have phenomenal hearing so that he can hear a wild turkey gobble and distinguish the distance and direction from which the gobble has come.

... be able to tell from years of experience which way a gobbling turkey is facing on the roost, whether a turkey is gobbling from a high ridge or down in a valley and if there's any thick cover between him and the turkey.

... have the stalking skills of a cat and the speed of a cheetah to move to a turkey without spooking the keen-sighted tom.

... have the eyesight of an eagle to see the white crown of a gobbler's head at 50 or 60 yards, the tips of a bird's fanned tail or the feet of a gobbler 30 or 40 yards away when the bird is strutting behind a fallen tree.

... have the endurance of a wild mustang.

... be able to call, stalk, run, climb and pursue a turkey from before daylight until the closing rays at dusk.

... have the ability to go without food and water and often without protection from the elements.

... be a man of strong resolution who will stand firm in his commitment to bag a gobbler, even when lesser men give up.

... have an inner spirit that allows him to overcome the many defeats and disappointments he will surely experience.

... realize that even when he's victorious, on the following hunt he's more likely to strike out than he is to hit a home run with a turkey.

... be an accurate shot and know the effective range of his gun and shot—under all circumstances.

... be able to judge distance with the precision of a professional golfer.

... be able to combine all of these skills effortlessly.

Taking A Turkey

The hunter:

1) Clothes himself from head to toe in camouflage.

2) Hears a turkey gobble.

3) Slips to within 75-100 yards of the turkey without the turkey seeing him.

4) Sits next to a tree that's larger than his shoulders.

5) Makes two or three yelps on his box call.

6) Puts the box down.

7) Places his shotgun on his knee.

8) Points the gun toward the direction from where the turkey called.

9) Waits until the turkey walks to within 30 yards, and he has a clear shot at the turkey's head, which is sticking straight up and standing perfectly still.

10) Looks down his gun barrel, superimposes the bead on his shotgun on the spot where the turkey's neck joins his body and squeezes the trigger.

11) Walks over to the gobbler, picks the bird up by his feet and carries the bronze baron out of the woods to dinner.

Although this scenario is how turkey hunting should be, wily, feathered woods wizards often don't read the same rule book that hunters do. They play the game by an altogether different set of rules.

How Turkey Dodge Hunters

The turkey's rule book for dodging hunters reads:

1) Anything that moves on the forest floor is the enemy.

2) Every thicket has a predator in it.

3) Anything you see and don't understand is dangerous.

4) Any sound that you can't recognize is life-threatening.

5) Don't go to any hen that you don't see.

6) A hunter is sneaking around in the woods trying to kill you from the time you first see daylight.

7) The hunter may be perceptive, but he's probably slow of mind and foot.

Turkey hunting is a game of strategy, of moves and counter moves. You're playing against one of the smartest critters to walk the forest floor.

8) Once you recognize there's a hunter in the woods, keep your mouth shut, your eyes open, your wings prepared for take-off and your feet ready to sprint at a moment's notice.

9) As long as there's cover between you and the hen, she's supposed to come to you, and let you see her before she sees you.

10) You may end up on some hunter's dinner table if you allow your sex drive to overpower your survival instincts.

11) You can make another move that will save your life for every move the hunter initiates.

When the Game Begins

Now that we know what rules the hunter and the turkey will follow, we need to look at the strategies that most contestants use to play the game. One of the best ways to understand the strategies of any game is to have them explained by an expert. Here's what

Ben Rodgers Lee, a world champion turkey caller, has to say: "Most turkey hunting strategies begin with locating the bird, because the hunter wants to hear a turkey gobble to signify the beginning of the game. But in many areas, turkey won't gobble or will gobble very little for several reasons, including that the morning is overcast, rainy or cold.

"In some parts of the country where turkey have been hunted hard for many years, sportsmen are responsible for breeding turkey that won't gobble or gobble very little. If the hunters kill off the good gobbling turkey every spring, the turkey that gobble the least survive the longest and breed the hens. If gobbling is a trait that can be passed on, then the toms that gobble the least will pass this trait on to their progeny. In each generation of turkey, the ones that gobble the most usually will be the ones that are harvested."

If the birds don't gobble, a turkey hunter will find locating a turkey to hunt very difficult. There are some tactics to use in this situation.

1) Blow either a crow or hawk call to shock a tom into gobbling, which is a reaction similar to what you have if someone jumps out from behind a bush at your home in the dark and screams. Although you may not be able to speak, you will involuntarily make a sound like, "Yowl!" The turkey's shock gobble will help you locate him.

2) Position yourself where a turkey should show up or has shown up in the past. Walk around or crawl through thick cover separating you from where you expect a turkey to be so you won't spook the bird. Or wait until the next morning and attempt to get on the same side of the thicket as he is before he flies down from the roost. If you can position yourself between the turkey's roost tree and where he wants to go after he flies down from the roost, you can bag him whether he talks or not.

3) Locate another likely-looking place to find a tom, or hunt later in the morning. Often if a bird won't gobble by daylight, he may gobble later in the day.

4) If a tom won't answer a hen, try a gobbling call. He might challenge a rival gobbler. Always sit with your back against a tree that's wider than your shoulders. When you make a gobbling sound, you might be hunted by an inexperienced sportsman.

5) Pray for an act of God to spook that closed-mouth gobbler to you.

Just as in chess where you must lay a trap for your opponent, you must lay a trap for the turkey. To lay a trap for a tom, sit in a hardwood forest with a tree to your back and no underbrush between you and the turkey. Then the turkey can walk to you, and you can bag him.

Sometimes the game works this way but more often it doesn't.

The best way to take a turkey is to be where he wants to walk, which is relatively easy if you've pre-scouted and spent time learning the habits of this particular opponent. But if this is the first time you've met the bird you plan to hunt, you probably won't know where he wants to go. Let's examine possible strategies you can use.

If there's no big tree to sit down next to, you can use a portable blind to set in front of you so that the turkey won't spot you. If you didn't bring a portable blind, you either can sit inside a stump hole, off the edge of a bank or in front of the roots of a blown-down tree. Don't sit in the top of a cut-down tree, in a bush or hide behind thick cover. The turkey expects danger to lurk in thick places. You may have to sit next to two small trees, lay down flat on the ground or stand beside a tree to take the bird.

"If there's not a tree big enough to sit down beside without showing my silhouette, I remain standing and lean up against a tree. I think a turkey may assume that I'm just another tree growing beside a real tree," says Don Taylor, an experienced turkey hunter.

If you can't find a place to call a gobbler to without being seen, another tactic is to circle the turkey until you find a large tree in a clear woods.

Getting A Turkey To Come To You

Generally, all a hunter must do is take either a box call or a push-button call, make a few soft yelps and wait for the turkey. However, when the gobbler doesn't answer or come to you, use a different call.

Just because you've selected the best instrument to play the love tune of a hen turkey does not ensure that you will call the bird to you. The older a turkey, the stranger he will be. Remember, a turkey's rule book specifies that the tom is to play the game by gobbling and the hen will come to him. You're trying to get that bird to commit an unnatural act. He's gobbling and you're answering like a hen turkey, but you're not going to him.

Some smart, proud gobblers will walk, strut, drum and display 75 to 80 yards away from where they think the hen is. These birds are like the muscle-bound beach bums who lean up against picnic tables and show off their biceps and triceps. These guys get to thinking, "I'm so good-looking that every woman on this beach wants to be with me. If that girl doesn't come over to where I am, I'm surely not going to move over to where she is."

Once you understand that that's the kind of bird you're fooling with, you must start playing the game according to his rules. Counter his move like a good-looking woman in a string bikini with sun-bleached hair and a golden tan might tantalize the muscle-bound beach boy. Act disinterested in the turkey's display. Accomplish that by *not calling*. Or, if you do call, give light purrs and clucks to let him know where you are but to show that you're not interested in what he's doing. Many times this will hurt the gobbler's pride and make him think, "That hen doesn't really see how beautiful my feathers are." Then you can take that tom when he comes in to give that hen a closer look.

If this tactic doesn't work, let the turkey cool down and walk off. Because he's been strutting and drumming, you know that he's ready to mate. Once the gobbler is out of sight, get up, circle the turkey, change calls and start talking to him again. Now he'll think there's another hen interested in meeting him. Since he's already hot and bothered, he may come quickly to this new hen with lovemaking on his mind.

If this technique doesn't pay off, return the next morning and move to within 20 yards of where he strutted and drummed the morning before. Take a stand. Since the tom feels safe and comfortable in that spot, he'll probably return to this same region to strut and drum again. But this time you'll be close enough to take him.

If that technique doesn't work, go to the turkey the next morning and after he gobbles call to him with a few yelps. When he gobbles once more, call to him again. Then get up and leave before the turkey reaches the area. Use this routine three mornings in a row.

Then on the fourth morning, don't leave. Often the turkey will come running in to where you are, because for three mornings in a row when the hen has called, he's answered and made a date. But his lady love has left each time. The bird might assume that since he hasn't said anything to offend her, the only reason she has left is that another gobbler has come in and taken her before he's arrived. So on the fourth morning, he'll sprint to his lady love.

Bringing a gobbler in this close takes experience. But practice, patience and dedication can result in some close encounters.

After You've Called The Bird

After you have the gobbler's attention, he should come walking straight to you. When he's at 30 yards, shoot him. But · remember that's not the way the tom always plays the game. Many times there won't be any reason in the world that a turkey shouldn't walk straight to where you are. But instead he will come up from the side. That's when you have one of three options. Option number one: Jump up, turn sideways and shoot. Rarely does a hunter ever outdraw a turkey. Your odds of successfully using this strategy are slim, very slim. Option two: Slide around the tree to face the bird. This may be the best tactic. But often the turkey will spot you when you move. Option three: Wait for the turkey to walk in front of you, which is usually the best decision to make.

If the turkey doesn't walk up beside you or doesn't come straight to you, there's only one other way the bird can get from where he is to where you are. He may walk up behind you. If this occurs, you have several courses of action, but all are blind strategies.

You can jump up, spot the bird and shoot. Or, you can hope the bird can't see you, roll away from the tree and onto your stomach. If he doesn't spot your move, you can take a shot from a prone position. Your visibility is greatly reduced when you're lying on your stomach, and your ability to point the gun at the turkey is restricted when you're lying prone rather than sitting up. Finally, you can remain motionless until the turkey walks in front of you. If he hasn't spotted you, he shouldn't. When the turkey comes up this close, your ability to remain motionless may not help you win the game, but it will prevent you from losing the game.

If you can't get the turkey to walk in front of you, the best tactic is to realize that you're in a stand-off. If both sides walk away, you can return and play the game another day with this same tom without teaching him a new strategy.

However, if you move and the turkey observes you, you've taught him another trick in dodging hunters. He'll be more difficult to call the next time you meet him. But if he doesn't see you and assumes that the hen walked off before he arrived, you may be able to return to that same site the following morning, take a stand in a different place and call the old boy in.

How, Where and When To Shoot

This portion of the game should be the easiest.

1) All of your strategies have worked.
2) The bird has fallen into your trap.
3) Now all you must do is take him.
4) However, this is when most hunters defeat themselves.

There are three common mistakes that hunters make when the bird is within gun range. First, they misjudge the effective killing distance of their firearm. Since gobblers are big birds, they often appear to be closer to the hunter in the woods than they actually are. If you don't predetermine your killing range before you see a turkey, you probably won't down the gobbler.

Pick four or five trees in various locations around your stand as markers. Decide that if the turkey doesn't come inside that ring of trees you won't shoot. Instead you will wait and hunt the bird another day. If he does come into your effective area, be prepared to take the shot.

The second mistake that a hunter makes in shooting a turkey is that he doesn't get his cheek down on the stock, look straight down the gun barrel and superimpose the bead on the turkey's head. This hunter is looking so intensely at the turkey that he forgets the correct shooting position. Therefore, before you squeeze the trigger, always ask yourself: Do I feel the stock against my cheek? Can I see the bead at the end of the barrel? Can I see the bead on the turkey's head? Now squeeze.

Even when you go this far in your checklist of shooting, there's still the third mistake; lack of a clean shooting lane. Even in clean woods, oftentimes that turkey will manage to place a vine, small sapling or some kind of brush between you that you may not see. Even a limb the diameter of a quarter that's hanging in front of the turkey's head can absorb all the shot that was intended for the bird's neck. Therefore just before you squeeze the trigger, make sure there's no obstacle between the bead of the shotgun and the turkey's head.

Once The Turkey Is Down

One Alabama hunter was so proud of the gobbler that he had just shot that he laid his shotgun down beside the turkey, took his camera out of his coat pocket and took a picture. While he was putting his camera back in his coat pocket, the turkey, apparently only stunned, jumped up and ran off. This hunter has a picture of the turkey he shot, but he's yet to eat his turkey dinner.

Sometimes when a turkey goes down, he may only be stunned because the pellets didn't penetrate his brain or neck. Therefore as

To leave the woods with a gobbler over your shoulder, ask yourself these questions before you pull the trigger: Do I feel the stock against my cheek? Can I see the bead at the end of the barrel? Can I see the bead on the turkey's head?

soon as you shoot, run to the turkey. If you don't, the bird may run away from you. Once you get to the gobbler, put the heel of your boot on the tom's head, grab the bird's feet and pull upward.

Although you have the turkey, the game is still not over. You have several options for getting the bird out of the woods. You can throw the tom over your shoulder, but after 50 to 100 yards, that 17-18 pound bird will feel as though he's put on 30 pounds. The turkey will feel even heavier on your shoulder than he looked on his own two feet. After you've lugged that bird one-half mile, that 18 pound gobbler seems to weigh at least 75 pounds. Either carry a turkey sling or a vest to make getting the bird out of the woods easier.

Turkey hunting is a game of strategies, moves and counter moves. It is played by the smartest critter that walks the forest floor.

Factors That Make Turkey Tough To Take

When a hunter is unable to bag a gobbler, he can come up with all types of excuses to explain why the turkey in his area are tougher to take than turkey anywhere else. I know, because I've used all those excuses myself. There are, however, some legitimate reasons why turkey are tougher to take in some areas.

The permit system that a state uses for turkey season often determines how hard the birds are to bag. For instance, in states where there are a limited number of permits, hunters will often have a more difficult task than sportsmen in states with unlimited permits.

To understand why this makes such a difference, we must realize the mind of a turkey hunter during turkey season. That's often as critical to a hunter's success as outthinking or outmaneuvering a turkey.

Let's analyze a sportsman named Joe who lives in a state where a drawing determines who will hunt wild turkey. Let's assume that Joe's state permits the harvesting of 1,000 spring gobblers, but that there are an average of 8,000 applicants. So only one in eight applicants will receive a permit. Although Joe has applied for a turkey permit for the two previous seasons, he has not been drawn. But this season, luck is with Joe as he is the 827th name drawn.

To ensure his success, Joe starts scouting for turkey. Not only does he ride the roads listening for a turkey to gobble, he also spends every spare minute and all of his days off scouting the area. Joe realizes that to be successful he must pinpoint the exact

In much of North America, gobblers can be found near the edge of fields that are close to woodlots. This is also a good spot to take a stand during the middle of the day.

location of a specific gobbler and try to get to know that gobbler on a first name basis well before the season begins.

Joe knows that the crow call, the hawk call and the owl hooter are the best calls to find gobblers without giving away his position. However, when he fails to hear a responding gobble after using these calls, he reaches into his hunting coat and commits the unpardonable sin of pulling out a turkey call. It may be a box, slate or mouth diaphragm call. Although Joe will tell himself that he just wants to use this call to pinpoint where a turkey is, deep within his soul he realizes that he is trying to call that turkey so he can get a look at the bird before the season opens.

Joe has been practicing with that turkey call for three years. It's tough for him to refrain from testing his skills and engaging in verbal combat with a gobbler to prove his prowess. Although Joe realizes he shouldn't be calling, much less educating a turkey before the season, he still wants to work that gobbler just to know that he can. He'll also attempt to learn as much as he can about that turkey before the season opens.

If we multiply Joe by the 1,000 hunters in that permit state, almost every one will be familiarizing the gobblers with a turkey call and training the toms to dodge hunters. These gobblers soon learn what a turkey call sounds like. More than likely they'll have several hunter encounters before the season open. Even though the turkey population may be small, many will be call-shy and hunter-smart before the opening day of turkey season.

To improve his chances of filling his tag, Joe should leave his turkey call at home. If need be, he should lock them in a safe and give the key to a friend who will not return it until opening morning.

When scouting before the opener, Joe should take a crow call, hawk call and an owl call into the woods. That's it. Then if he does find a turkey, he won't be tempted to call and educate the tom.

Flatlander In The Open Spaces

A turkey is much like the cockroach in that it can adapt to almost any type of terrain, climate or weather condition.

For many NAHC members, hunting the eastern turkey is the traditional method of harvesting wild turkey. Even the Oceola turkey is not that much different in his habits and habitat than the eastern turkey.

But when an eastern hunter goes West, he finds an altogether different hunting situation. Western turkey in many regions don't even act as though they are of the same feather as the eastern birds. For instance, the Rio Grande turkey near Sonora, Texas have two speeds—stop and trot. In the East, turkey walk, trot, run, fly and hang out. But when Rio Grande birds leave the roost to find food, water, shade or sex, they move at a fast trot.

One of the keys to bagging Rio Grande gobblers is to learn where and when they go for water, and which small scrub oak thickets they use to dodge the sun. That way, if a hunter is unable to bag a turkey going to food or water, he may still bag a tom by taking a stand where the bird seeks shelter. However, the traditional eastern tactic of calling to the gobbler while he's on his roost is not nearly as effective as taking a stand between the turkey's roost and water hole, roost and feed, or roost and shade tree.

In New Mexico, hunters learn about hunting at high altitudes while chasing Merriam gobblers across the Rocky Mountains. In Alabama, although the turkey may roost on a mountain, they'll usually spend most of their days on the top of a mountain or in the hollows between the mountains. These eastern turkey are not very enthusiastic about walking across mountains.

Merriam birds, meanwhile, will gobble once and then walk across at least three ridges before gobbling a second time. Because of the open spaces of the West, the distance from the hunter to the turkey can be deceiving. Hunters who hear a turkey gobble sometimes swear he's only 100 yards away. However, the gobbler is usually three-quarters of a mile away, on some distant ridge. The key to hunting Merriam gobblers that live above the rimrock is proper conditioning by the hunter. These Merriam birds survive on much less oxygen than eastern birds. It's a humbling experience when the eastern hunter attempts to do the same. High altitude hunting brings even the toughest eastern gobbler chaser to his knees.

Although many turkey experts believe that the Merriam gobbler is the easiest to take—primarily because these birds have not been exposed to as much hunting pressure as eastern birds—the sportsman who goes after one must be in excellent physical condition.

Turkey hunters have waded chest-deep swamp water in the South to reach a turkey on a small island in the middle of flooded timber. They've sprinted the deserts of Texas to get ahead of those fast-trotting Rio Grande birds. They've hauled themselves up the sides of the Rocky Mountains in pursuit of Merriam gobblers.

The high-altitude home of the Merriam gobbler can make for a physically demanding hunt. In addition to the foothills of the Rocky Mountains, this bird can be found in the South and Midwest.

Few, if any of these hunters will claim that one species is "easy" to take.

Each species requires a different technique; and the birds in every region of the country call for some degree of specialization. But this is what makes turkey hunting such an interesting sport. Just about the time the sportsman thinks he has learned all he can learn, hunted everywhere he can hunt and done battle with every type of turkey known to man, out pops a gobbler that breaks the rules and eludes his every effort.

3

Getting Ready
For The Turkey Season

The worst way to begin the turkey season is to wait until the night before to get your equipment together. Here are the results:

When you attempt to put on those size 34 pants that you bought two seasons before, they won't wrap around the 36-inch waist. Actually, the pants can be forced to the straining point, however, a belt won't fit through the belt loops. And wearing a pair of pants that are too small for a day of turkey hunting is uncomfortable and unnecessary.

Another problem in waiting until the last minute is that you realize the gremlin that gets into your hunting gear and steals important items has returned for a visit. That gremlin always steals one polypropylene sock or the peg for your slate call. He gnaws a hole in the knee of your pants or long underwear. Typically he hides at least one important piece of equipment.

Therefore, here's a system that will serve you well. During February, long before turkey season starts, pack your gear. Take a large tote bag and pack it as though you're leaving the next morning. Try on all your clothes and make a list of what you need. Test your calls and make sure they function properly.

Next, make a list of the gear you'll need, like shotgun shells, candy bars, matches and underwear. Then, three weeks before turkey season, go to the store and buy that equipment. When the

Pre-season scouting trips are a good time to talk out hunting strategies and reminisce about hunts gone by.

season arrives, you'll know that all you need to do is pick up your bag and head for camp.

Getting your supplies together is the easy part. Getting yourself together requires more time and energy.

Physical Preparation

The ability to hunt hard all day is often the difference between success and failure. Physical conditioning is a must if you want to enjoy the sport. It's that simple.

When most people start a conditioning program one of the biggest problems is a conviction that their bodies should be pushed to the limit each time they exercise. Avoid this conviction.

Your body is not ready for maximum stress at the beginning of a conditioning program. The human body can be damaged if too much stress is inflicted on it from the beginning. Any good

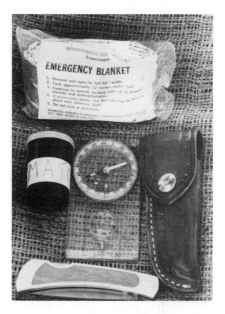

One of the first pieces of equipment to check each year is your survival kit. At a minimum, it should include a survival blanket, matches, compass and knife.

conditioning program begins with a medical examination. Then it starts with light exercise to give the body a base on which to build a conditioning program. As the body becomes stronger, it can withstand more stress to develop and become stronger.

Although most turkey hunters realize that their legs are what will carry them to the gobblers, it's wrong to assume that leg conditioning is the most important part of your training. The circulatory and respiratory systems play a far greater role. A long walk or quick sprint to a turkey may result in an adverse effect on your body if it is not prepared for this rigorous exercise. And don't forget your back and shoulder muscles. Many turkey hunters will carry 20 to 40 pounds of gear for several miles. If they're lucky enough to bag a 15- to 20-pound gobbler, add that to the weight of the clothes, calls, rainsuit and other gear. *Your body must be conditioned to carry this load if the hunt is to be enjoyable.*

Begin with a walking program six to eight weeks before the turkey season. Remember to throw in some push-ups, toe touches, sit-ups and other general exercises.

Walk 30 to 45 minutes on level ground every day. During the second week, concentrate on walking up and down hills. By the third week, you'll probably be in good enough shape to start a jogging/walking program that covers one to three miles every day.

Although you're not training to be an Olympic athlete, you don't want poor physical condition to prohibit you from taking a turkey. Continue at this one- to three-mile pace until the season arrives.

This conditioning program is primarily for the flatland hunter. However, if you're planning to hunt at high altitudes, intensify your jogging program. After several weeks of general conditioning, concentrate on walking or running up and down steps. Also spend at least one or two days in camp prior to the hunt to become acclimated to the higher altitudes.

I never understood the difference between hunting turkey above sea level and hunting southern turkey in Alabama. But when I went to New Mexico and chased Merriam gobblers across the Rocky Mountains at 8,000 feet, I realized that my conditioning program was lacking in high altitude training. Although I hunted turkey at home and walked up to 10 miles per day, running across those mountains and chasing turkey made my legs feel as limp as if I kicked my way across the Atlantic. My mind was in high gear and emotionally I was running at full throttle, but my body was moving in slow motion. I learned that my conditioning program would have to change if I hunted high altitude gobblers.

Prepare your body for turkey hunting. This sport can be strenuous. Also, have a complete physical before the season. Nobody likes to admit that they're in poor physical condition, but only a fool will put his body under the physical stress of turkey hunting without first having a complete check-up.

A complete check-up should also include an eye exam. Your eyesight is as critical to your success as a gobbler's eyesight is to his survival. Having your eyes checked, and wearing glasses if needed, will increase your odds of bagging a bird.

Just as important as preparing your clothes and body is cleaning, oiling and testing your shotgun. Make sure all parts function properly. A safety that sticks, an automatic that fails to eject or a slide on a pump that malfunctions, can turn a promising hunt into disappointing failure. Assume that anything that possibly can go wrong will go wrong. Check everything.

4

The Complete
Turkey Hunter

The bronze baron of the spring woods can be harvested without using the latest, state of the art equipment. However, you don't have to be miserable to hunt the wild turkey. Using better equipment means you will hunt more comfortably, and perhaps more successfully. You'll also derive more satisfaction from the sport of gobbler chasing. First let's dress the turkey hunter. Then we'll equip him.

Caring For Your Feet

The turkey hunter lives or dies on his feet, so proper footwear is critical to a successful hunt. Since the sportsman may have to walk, run or wade, he must have footgear that can get him through, around and over whatever type of terrain he encounters.

Start with a pair of polypropylene sock liners. These will keep your feet warm and dry. If your feet get sweaty in the process of walking to the calling area, polypropylene sock liners will wick the moisture away from feet and keep them warmer. On top of the sock liner, wear either a cotton or wool sock, depending on the temperature in which you're hunting.

Many sportsmen prefer innersoles inside their boots. Innersoles are pads that cushion the feet against the punishment of long walks, steep climbs and rocky terrain. Keeping the hunter's feet comfortable is much like having the proper tires on an automobile.

A turkey hunter lives or dies on his feet. That's why a good pair of boots, like Browning's Nomad Goretex, are required equipment.

If you have the best vehicle in the world, but the tires give way, the vehicle is out of commission. The same is true of the turkey hunter. If his feet are not warm, dry and comfortable, he's headed for a world of misery.

The turkey hunter's feet are warm, but to keep them that way and give them added support we'll need a good pair of hunting boots. How a boot feels on your foot is often the most important question when selecting boots. But you'll also want to look for a quality, waterproof pair that is lightweight, yet still provides good arch support.

If possible, buy a boot with a Vibram, rather than a lug, sole. Vibrams will grip just as well in rough conditions, and you won't end up "lugging" as much mud around with you.

If you're worried about snakes when hunting turkey, buy a pair of knee-high boots. Any hunter who constantly watches for snakes on the forest floor, won't be able to spot the turkey that might be sneaking toward his spot.

Some turkey hunters prefer to wear tennis shoes. Although they may be light and quiet, tennis shoes don't provide much support. Nor can they keep your feet warm or dry. Avoid tennis shoes. Invest in a good pair of boots.

Actually the avid turkey hunter may need two pairs of boots, because rarely will a turkey gobble on the same side of the creek. Most creeks will be over boot-top high. No boot will protect your foot and keep it dry when water pours over the top of it. Bring two pairs: one to wade streams and the other for hiking.

The sole of the boot is one area that many hunters fail to camouflage. Often, a hunter will sit for long periods of time with his feet stretched straight out from the tree. If the sportsman has light-colored soles on his boots, those soles will appear like a red light blinking in the night. When a gobbler comes in, he'll see the soles of the boots and be alerted.

Material And Camo Patterns That Work

Now that we've readied the feet let's dress the torso, beginning with 100 percent polypropylene underwear for its ability to wick moisture away from the skin.

When a hunter is considering which camo pattern is best for him, he must remember that terrain usually dictates the color needed to disguise the hunter. Depending on who you talk to, a strong case can be made for almost every camo pattern.

Roy Moyer is 97 years old and a veteran turkey hunter. He says, "I just bought me a gray work shirt and gray work pants and took brown paint and dabbed it over the pants and shirt. That camo suit always has worked well for me." Other hunters spend a great deal of time mixing and matching camo. Sometimes not only the area and the terrain dictate the camo pattern, but in some instances the individual bird you're hunting will help you decide what camo pattern is best.

Here's why: Some turkeys are experts at dodging hunters. Not only can they distinguish the hunter's calling, but they seem to have the ability to recognize a hunter's silhouette when he's leaning up against a tree. Some birds can more easily spot certain types of camo patterns. These are not ordinary gobblers but rather super-sharp toms that have been hunted for several years.

One of the best tactics to hide from the turkey is to mix and match camo. For instance, some hunters who specialize in taking these ornery, old gobblers will use a vertical pattern like Trebark or Realtree for their shirt, jacket and headnet, and then wear either a leaf or woodland green pattern for their pants. Then the pants will

When you consider which camouflage to buy for turkey hunting, remember that terrain often dictates which color and style works best.

blend in with the leafy forest floor, and their torsos will vanish into the tree's bark.

Much of the time the turkey hunter will be leaning against a tree, therefore the camo pattern that most resembles the trunk of a tree seems to be the most logical pattern. This is why patterns like Trebark, Realtree, Mossy Oak and Woodhide have become so popular in recent years.

If you're hunting turkey in a pine forest, a vertical pattern may be the best camouflage. Even when a tree is blown down a vertical pattern is best and not out of place in a pine forest. However, if you're hunting in a forest with mixed age timber, there often will be bushes and shrubs growing on the forest floor below the timber. So a leaf or forest green pattern may be best for the springtime hunter.

The new patterns that combine vertical camo with a leaf pattern give the hunter the best of both worlds. The Realtree leaf pattern in most instances is appropriate in southern forests. The Trebark pattern works extremely well not only in forests but also in mountainous and rocky terrain. Even though matching the camo pattern to the terrain may not be as critical as some turkey hunters believe, try and use the camo that is most like the terrain. In snow country, use a white camo pattern that mixes white with brown to blend in with the surroundings.

Never appear as a solid color against a mixed color background. Breaking up your silhouette is one of the critical keys to good camouflage. Pin-on leaves from Realtree are an excellent way to break up your silhouette. Although a sportsman in full camouflage with plastic pin-on leaves resembles a bull at a tea party, when he slips into the woods and moves through the forest he becomes virtually invisible.

One problem with camouflage is that sometimes hunting buddies dictate what you should and should not wear. When I first started pinning leaves on my camo suit, I was the joke of the hunting camp. But when the other hunters saw how I vanished into the woods, they started saying, "Hey, John, how about letting me borrow a few of those leaves? That stuff just may work."

There are different thicknesses of both shirts and pants for the turkey hunter. Some people believe that wearing thinner garments will help them keep cooler during the spring. However, mosquitoes penetrate light clothing even though you're wearing insect repellent. Those long-nosed demons of destruction can drill right through your pants leg and into your hide. Wear the heavier material. Don't wear a short-sleeved shirt under a camo netting jacket, even when the weather is hot. One trip to the swamps will convince any turkey hunter that putting up with heavier material, although a little warmer, is worth the trouble.

Also, purchase a quiet, camouflaged rainsuit for turkey hunting in foul weather.

Camouflaging Your Head

When I was a small boy, I enjoyed playing cowboys and Indians. I always wanted to be an Indian, because I liked to put on war paint. I thought I looked good with streaks of red, yellow and black over my face, arms and chest. Everybody, even people who weren't playing the game, realized I was the Indian.

So naturally when I first started turkey hunting, I used camo grease paint. Then everyone recognized me as a turkey hunter when I walked into a country store to pick up provisions for camp. I used the rationale that without the obstruction of a headnet I could hear and see better. However, I soon remembered that mosquitoes bite, even through the most potent insect repellent. So I gave up my grease paint for a full headnet.

For a comfortable day afield, spray the headnet with 100 percent deet insect repellent and then let the net air out for a minute before putting it on. The insect repellent will keep the mosquitoes not only from penetrating the netting, but also far enough away from your ears so that they don't sing to you while you're trying to concentrate on a turkey. You might even feel more camouflaged with a headnet. There are few, if any, drawbacks to a headnet.

Don't put your eyeglasses on under a headnet until you've cooled down. A headnet traps heat and will fog glasses. If you must wear glasses while you're walking to where you want to set up, purchase some anti-fogging liquid at a camera store. Photographers use this chemical to keep their lens clean and fog free. It will do the same job on your eyeglasses.

Camouflaging Your Hands

Having the proper gloves is important to the turkey hunter because the hands will move more than any other part of the body when the turkey is at close range. Gloves are available in all types of camo patterns and material.

Cloth gloves are preferred by many hunters because when the mornings are cool they camouflage your hands and keep them warm. Some hunters prefer to wear heavy cotton work gloves in

The proper gloves are vitally important to the turkey hunter. Many hunters prefer wool or cotton gloves with the fingers cut off, because they keep the hands warm and fingers free for calling.

camo patterns with the fingers cut out. These gloves are also useful in the winter or fall. Have two or three different types of gloves, not only to match camo patterns but also to match different weather conditions.

For instance, in the desert where there are no mosquitoes, wear the net type gloves. In the swamps and hills wear cloth gloves. In the winter wear the wool no-finger gloves.

What Bug Juice Is Best?

Good clothing and netting won't always stop the hard-driving nose of a sharp-billed mosquito. Among others, Ben's 100, Deep Woods Off or Cutter's Insect Repellent are effective. The major consideration when buying insect repellent is to make sure that the repellent you use contains 100 percent deet. It will be tough to concentrate on the turkey in front of you if mosquitoes are buzzing around your head, redbugs are burying into your hide and ticks are crawling up your back. Therefore, spray yourself from head to toe with insect repellent. A warning: Be careful when using this type of repellent, because if you fail to let it dry before you handle your shotgun, it may take the finish off the gun.

Why Protect Your Fanny?

Another mandatory piece of equipment is a turkey seat which can make a long sit on the hard ground comfortable and increase the sportsman's odds of bagging a bird. The hunter's ability to sit still is directly related to his fanny's ability to stay comfortable. Other than insects, fanny fatigue causes more hunters to fidget and move than any other factor.

But a cushion is not the only way to eliminate fanny fatigue.

Before you sit down, be sure there are no rocks, limbs, sticks or stumps on the ground. A turkey chaser can get so excited when he's calling that he'll sit down quickly beside a tree before realizing that he's sitting on something that's causing extreme discomfort. The hunter either has to endure the pain or move and risk spooking the bird.

Use some type of cushion. The hunter with a turkey seat can wait motionlessly as long as is required for a gobbler to come in. Also, by having a comfortable seat, the sportsman can concentrate on shooting when the tom presents himself and not have his concentration broken by the discomfort of an object under his bottom.

Why should a hunter endure discomfort when he can use products that will prevent pain and discomfort and make his hunting more effective? Use products that make you more comfortable, it's that simple.

Essential Equipment

There are several other items that are essential for the turkey hunter:

Rangefinder. A rangefinder is a teaching aid that enables you to more accurately determine distances. By guessing the distance and then checking that distance with a rangefinder, a hunter can teach himself to be a more accurate judge of distances. When you sit down to call a turkey, use the rangefinder to measure the distance you are from different trees and bushes. When the turkey comes in and passes by those objects, you will know the distance to the gobbler. From patterning your shotgun, you will know your effective range.

Compass. Turkey hunters are notorious for getting lost in the woods. When turkey hunters hear a turkey gobble, the first reaction is to get to him as quickly as possible, set up and be ready to take the bird when he flies off the roost. But if you move several times during the hunt, you may not know where you are when the time comes to leave the woods.

When a turkey gobbles, look at your compass and determine the direction to the turkey and where that is in relation to your

A rangefinder is almost a necessity for today's turkey hunter. But don't use it to determine the distance to an animal. Instead, use it to determine distances to inanimate objects. Then when an animal walks past that tree or rock, you'll immediately know how far away he is.

vehicle. Not only have turkey hunters been lost while chasing turkey, but they've also had to return to the woods after dark to help find friends. A compass is essential.

Flashlight. Turkey hunters often go into the woods before daylight and come out of the woods after dark. A small flashlight can help the hunter's navigation through the woods. Keep your flashlight packed with your turkey hunting gear and only remove it to check the batteries.

Fanny Pack. With all the gear a turkey hunter carries into the woods, he can easily load up his pockets. The answer is to wear a fanny pack to store turkey calls, flashlight, compass and other gear. When you need any of the gear in the fanny pack, simply turn the pack to the front, take out the gear and slide the pack back. These lightweight packs can store a large amount of gear.

Turkey Toter. Most of us have seen pictures of the proud hunter walking out of the woods with a big gobbler over one shoulder and his gun over the other. Although this makes a beautiful picture and one that we all hope to pose for at some time, this method of bringing the tom out of the woods works best when you only have a few hundred yards to go. But if you're hunting a gobbler deep in the woods, and you're successful in bagging him, having those bony legs across your shoulder and holding that weight in one hand gets tiring and old quickly. Packing a bird out doesn't have to be uncomfortable.

A turkey hunting vest not only provides numerous pockets and an easy way to carry plenty of gear, but it also has a turkey toter on the back.

With a portable blind, you can set up a stand almost anywhere. It's also a handy item to hide the fidgeting of that beginner hunter.

Use a turkey toter, a turkey vest or the strings that ordinarily hold your blind together to carry the bird. The advantage of wearing a turkey vest is that you can eliminate carrying a fanny pack, cushion and a turkey toter. Most good turkey vests have pockets that will store all the gear a turkey hunter can think of, plus they feature a built-in cushion and a big game bag on the back for carrying out the game. Turkey vests are popular because all your gear can be stored in that vest throughout the hunting season. When you're ready to go turkey hunting all you have to pack is camo clothing, boots, socks and your turkey vest. If you don't have some type of vest designed specifically for turkey hunting, purchase a turkey toter.

Blind. Although some avid turkey hunters don't use a blind, it's best to keep a blind with your hunting gear. A blind eliminates the need to have a perfect place to set up because a blind can be put up anywhere. A blind is also extremely effective if you are using a friction call, like a box or a slate. By hiding in a blind, you can call and watch the tom but the bird will be unable to see your hands move. A blind is also useful when hunting with novice hunters and children since sitting still for long periods of time for someone unaccustomed to sitting still can be miserable. With a blind, the novice can squirm around and get below the blind without spooking the turkey.

Calls. The most effective turkey hunters are those who master a variety of calls. Some carry a box call, slate call, pushbutton call, diaphragm call, crow call, hawk call, owl hooter and anything else they may need. Some turkey will respond best to one particular type of call, others another type.

Binoculars. A quality pair of binoculars is as essential to a turkey hunter as a comfortable pair of boots. A sportsman can use binoculars to spot a turkey at a distance and determine whether that bird is a gobbler or a hen. Lightweight, camouflaged binoculars with good resolution are required.

Snacks. An aggressive turkey hunter doesn't always get back to camp at mealtime. Missing breakfast, lunch and supper is common. Because turkey hunting can involve considerable physical exertion, bring food along. Granola bars or candy bars that won't melt can be packed in either a vest or a fanny pack. Also, never forget that turkey hunters can get lost. Think about it, talk about it. There's always the chance that you may be injured or have some other calamity befall you that results in a night spent in the woods. Food can make that experience much more comfortable.

Matches. A hunter should never be caught without matches in a waterproof container. Again, no one believes they'll have to spend the night in the woods, but a warm campfire is an added comfort to a bad situation.

5

The Turkey Hunter's Shotgun

Trying to decide what shotgun is best for turkey hunting is much like attempting to decide what pair of shoes will best fit the human race. Not only are there different sizes, but each person also has his own idea about how a gun, or shoe, must look, feel and fit.

However, what's most important in both shoes and shotguns is style. By that I don't mean the design of the gun. Instead, I mean the style of hunting that you will use to bag a gobbler. Webster describes style as, "The way or manner in which anything is done." There are many styles of harvesting gobblers.

There once was a turkey hunter by the name of Smiley Shaw. Smiley was of the opinion that if a hunter couldn't bring a gobbler to within 15 steps of the blind, then he didn't have the right to kill the bird. Other sportsmen, meanwhile, use rifles for hunting turkey, and are of the opinion that accurate shot placement is a vital part of the sport.

Therefore, each hunter's style dictates what firearm he uses. Let's look at shotguns for turkey hunting and their applications to the sport.

The one gun that many NAHC members considered to be the ultimate turkey gun when it was first introduced was the Ithaca Mag. 10. This lightweight cannon, which is capable of taking turkey at 60 yards, has a kick like a young mule and is almost as cumbersome to carry. However, it does extend the range that a hunter can bag a gobbler and it does bring down a tom quickly and efficiently.

Next in the order of power is the 12 gauge, three-inch magnum. Preferred by many turkey hunters, a three-inch magnum is effective out to 40 or 50 yards. However, if one errs in judging distance, that little extra velocity is a welcome advantage.

There are three 12 gauge, three-inch magnums that fit the requirements of most turkey hunters:

1) The Browning BAR. This five shot automatic has a longer barrel than the other two. When a turkey is at 35 yards or less, simply put the bead of the shotgun on the bird's neck and squeeze the trigger. The turkey will drop.

2) The Remington Model 1187 SP. With a 26-inch barrel, the 1187 was a breakthrough in turkey guns some years back. Today in its updated version, it has a dull finish on both the wood and the metal which prevents the bird from being spooked by the glare of the gun's finish. The SP also features a sling, which many laud as an absolute necessity for the hunter who moves around when chasing gobblers. You'll also appreciate the shorter barrel of the SP, which is easier and quicker to move. And turkey hunters have learned that the shorter barrels can be just as accurate as the longer barrels at the greater distances.

3) Winchester Special Turkey Gun. This Winchester 12 gauge is built on the Model 1300 pump action. It is a three-inch magnum shotgun with a beautiful laminated stock and forearm, ventilated rib barrel, sling and a smooth action. There is also a lifetime warranty on the Winchoke system of tubes—choked extra full, full and modified—against choke damage from using steel shot factory loads. The gun is relatively lightweight and has a little more recoil than the Browning or the Remington. However, the Winchester Special Turkey Gun is deadly.

From these three-inch magnums a hunter can step down to the traditional 2¾-inch 12 gauge or 16 gauge. As the amount of powder and shot decreases, so does the effective range of the gun. With all other factors equal, the 2¾-inch 12 gauge will not reach out as far as the three-inch magnum or the 10 gauge.

The 16 gauge requires the bird to be even closer for an effective kill. Although turkey hunters are quickly seeing the 16 gauge being replaced by larger 12 gauge guns, an old favorite of many hunters is still the Browning Sweet 16.

The closer a turkey hunter has to be with the lighter gauge guns, the more hunting and calling skills the sportsman must

The Winchester Special Turkey Gun manufactured by U.S. Repeating Arms is one of the newest entries on the turkey hunting scene. This three-inch pump shotgun with beautiful laminated wood and sling is a turkey hunter's dream.

possess. Allen Jenkins of Liberty, Mississippi, president of the M.L. Lynch Call Company, finds his sport not in the killing of the turkey but rather in the calling of the bird. When Jenkins squeezes the trigger, he wants the bird to be close. He takes pride in harvesting his turkey with a double-barreled 20 gauge.

When Jenkins brings a gobbler within 30 yards, he knows that bird is his. Whether Jenkins squeezes the trigger or not isn't nearly as important as his knowing that he can. On one hunt with Jenkins, we waited while a giant gobbler with a harem of hens walked to within 12 steps of the blind before Jenkins shot. In a novice's hands, smaller gauges can cause the wounding of more gobblers. But with experience and practice, even a double-barreled 20 gauge can be lethal.

Another school of thought says a hunter should learn to be proficient with the guns he already owns. There may be an old single shot 12 gauge in your closet that your great grandfather used for hunting turkey. Although the gun may be considered a relic rather than a hunting tool, you may find that if you fire it at a pattern board, that single shot 12 gauge may hold a pattern as tight at 30-40 yards as some modern shotguns. But as with all older guns, first have it examined by a competent gunsmith. Perhaps the 12 gauge 2¾- inch shotgun you use for duck, rabbit and birds will also prove to be an effective turkey gun. Before you go out and purchase a new shotgun to hunt turkey, pattern your guns on a pattern board and determine their effective range. Often the turkey gun you hope to own is already in your closet.

Terrain can also dictate the type of shotgun to use. In much of the South, hunters may not be able to see a turkey coming at a distance of more than 40 or 50 yards. By contrast, hunters out West may spot the gobbler half a mile away and may have to take longer shots. So there are numerous factors that combine to determine which turkey gun is best for you.

Any sportsman who's serious about turkey hunting will eventually hunt with other people and bring beginners and their families into the sport. Typically, an experienced turkey hunter will have at least three effective turkey guns.

Usually the first gun is the one the hunter himself hunts with and the second gun is one he loans to a friend or a beginner who is hunting with him. Then if the hunter calls up a turkey for the beginner, he knows that the gun the novice is shooting has the ability to bring down the bird. The third gun is what many call the insurance gun. If either of the first two guns fail to operate

Hunters often find that the turkey gun they hope for is already in their gun cabinet. A pump like this Remington 870 with full choke is perfect for turkey hunting.

To make turkey hunting even more sporting, some experienced turkey hunters prefer using a smaller gauge shotgun—like this double barreled 20 gauge.

properly, that backup shotgun keeps the hunter in the woods.

But the gun itself is only one of two important considerations when selecting your firearm. The second consideration is the choke of the gun. The choke controls the pattern that will be produced at varying distances. Most turkey hunters hunt with a full choke. Others prefer a full/full choke to produce the tightest possible pattern at the greatest distance.

A turkey's head is about the size of a clenched fist. At 20 to 40 yards, that's not a very big target. Obviously, you want as many pellets as possible to enter the bird's head and neck area. At 20 to 40 yards a full/full choke delivers that tight pattern.

However, there is a problem associated with a tight patterning shotgun. Inside 20 yards the pattern opens up very little. Therefore, you'll need to have a perfect shot inside 20 yards with a full/full choke.

6

Shotgun
Loads And Patterning

The water drained out of my boot as we listened to the bird strut and drum 70 yards away. Aaron sat 20 yards in front and to the left of me. Fully camouflaged, he was slouched down beside a big oak tree, gun at the ready. His chest rose and fell, much like an athlete's who has just finished a 440-yard sprint. Aaron was ready, but the big bird was 20 yards out of range.

We had heard the turkey gobble at daylight. He was on a wooded knoll 30 yards across a flooded acorn flat. So under the cover of darkness, we entered the water and waded from tree to tree. When we reached the knoll, Aaron sat in front of me. I took a stand behind him to call the bird.

The old gobbler was responsive. He had answered from the roost, and once he hit the ground there was steady gobbling. At first this looked like a textbook hunt. However, the tom hung up about 60 yards away and started gobbling and strutting. He wouldn't break his strut to respond to my calling. The gobbler put on a show right in front of Aaron.

Other NAHC members who have seen a giant gobbler perform a mating ritual to impress a hen will understand why Aaron was so excited and his breathing so heavy. Although Aaron had taken a couple of turkey, he had always hunted with a guide. I wondered if he would hold his shot until the turkey broke his strut and came in.

If the bird moved off, we could change positions and try to call him again.

Like a ventriloquist throwing his voice into a wooden dummy, I turned my head to the left and concentrated on a hickory tree 20 yards to the left and 10 yards back. I tried to call to that tree, hoping the tom would think the hen was calling from that spot.

Finally, the old bird dropped his strut and came toward Aaron. As he walked in somewhat stiff-legged, Aaron moved his head even tighter against the stock. His headnet moved in and out as his breathing sped up from the excitement.

When the turkey was 50 yards from Aaron, the gobbler alerted and craned his neck. However, he didn't look directly at Aaron or me. If we waited a few more minutes, the turkey would be within 30 or 40 yards—perfect range for Aaron. Suddenly, the woods exploded with a thunderous sound. There was a cloud of smoke and a flurry of wings. There was the stumbling and falling of the hunter, and the words, "Son of a gun! I can't believe I missed that bird!" The tom ran off. Aaron picked himself up from the ground. The icy wade across the waist-deep slough had been in vain.

"Aaron, the turkey was at 50 yards when you shot. If you had held your shot for another two or three minutes, the bird would have walked in to where we were."

"I swear, I thought that the bird was only 20 yards away," Aaron emphasized. "He looked as big as the side of a house. When his head went up and he alerted, I thought he would run off. I decided that if I didn't shoot, we wouldn't be able to take him."

When asked how tight his gun patterned at 50 yards, Aaron answered, "Well, I don't know. I've never shot it at that distance. Are you sure the bird was at 50 yards?"

After stepping off the distance, we found that Aaron had taken a 54-yard shot. Our hunt was over for that morning. But before we judge Aaron too severely, let's go back and look at what caused him to go home with an empty shell casing instead of a gobbler.

Judging Distance

Misjudging distance is easy when a hunter is unaccustomed to seeing a gobbler in the woods. When a tom is walking with his head erect he looks bigger than many people expect, thus giving the appearance of being closer than he really is. If the hunter can't accurately judge the distance he is from the bird, he'll be unable to determine the effectiveness of the shot once he squeezes the

Misjudging the distance to a gobbler is easy if you're unaccustomed to seeing one in the woods. This tom is walking with his head erect. He looks bigger, and thus closer, than he actually is. This bird is about 30 yards away.

trigger. Therefore, judging distance is the first step in understanding the patterning of your shotgun.

Even if you know the effective range of the gun—let's say out to 50 yards—if you misjudge the distance to the bird you'll be unsure whether your pattern will put enough pellets in the gobbler to bring him down. To be an efficient turkey hunter, develop a system of determining distances.

Ronnie Groom, a master hunter from Panama City, Florida, explains the system he uses to judge distance in the woods: "Since I played football in high school and college and enjoy watching it on TV, I know what 10 yards looks like. Therefore, when I'm in the woods, I try to determine where 10 yards is from my stand. Then from the end of that 10 yards, I attempt to decide where the next 10 yards ends, which lets me know exactly where 20 yards is from me. I continue building on that 10 yard base until I'm out to 60 yards. As I'm measuring off each 10 yard segment, I pick out a tree or bush that's at the end of each 10 yard division as a reference for when game passes that point."

Marlowe Larson, a nationally known field archer from Ogden, Utah, constantly shoots targets from 30-100 yards. And when he's hunting, he applies those field archery distances to the distances he must shoot when he's in the woods.

However, one of the best techniques to determine distances is to use a rangefinder. Some sportsmen assume that a rangefinder is used to determine the distance to the game. Once they learn the distance with the rangefinder, then they are ready to shoot. This is one way to use a rangefinder. It is not the most effective. The hunter who uses a rangefinder to judge the distances *to an animal* must bring the rangefinder to his eye, focus it on the target, read the distance, put the rangefinder back in his pocket, pick up his firearm and prepare for the shot. If the sportsman goes through that much movement, the game—especially a turkey—will spot the hunter and be spooked.

A better method is to use the rangefinder when you're *not* looking at game. As you walk through the woods, look at trees, bushes and stumps. Guess the distance. Then take the rangefinder, look at that same object and see how far away it is. The more you practice, the better you'll be at accurately judging distances.

Another way to use the rangefinder is to check the distance from your calling position to different objects in your field of view. When you sit down to call a gobbler, use the rangefinder to determine how far you are from a number of trees and bushes. Then make a mental decision not to take a shot at a gobbler if he doesn't walk into that effective area, which is typically 35 yards from your position. The three guns mentioned earlier are all effective at 35 yards. Tell yourself that if a tom doesn't come within that range, you'll wait until your next outing.

Never force a shot. If a gobbler doesn't move into your effective area, don't shoot. That requires mental and physical discipline. Letting a turkey walk off that's only 40 yards away is often more pressure than some hunters can stand. Experienced hunters, meanwhile, will let the turkey walk off, then move to a new calling position and begin to call again. Most of the time they're able to bring that same bird in closer to the new area.

A favorite game to play before and during hunting season is, "How Far Is The Turkey?" When walking with several buddies through the woods, one hunter points out a tree or bush and declares that to be the turkey. Everyone guesses the distance, and writes their guess on a piece of paper. Someone then uses a rangefinder to measure the distance. At the end of the hunt,

If you will be hunting with a partner, practice in the position that you intend to hunt. You'll learn how the gun handles from that position and develop the strength to hold it in that position.

everyone compares scores to determine how accurate each member is at judging distances. This game is excellent training for both the novice and experienced hunter.

It's surprising the amount of time turkey hunters spend practicing their calling and how little time they spend practicing judging distances. If a hunter calls in a turkey but doesn't know how far that turkey is from him before he squeezes the trigger, chances are he'll miss the bird.

Before you pattern your shotgun or decide which shells will shoot best in which guns, program yourself to become the best judge of distance you can be.

Patterning Your Shotgun

Some terms have different meanings to various hunters. For

some people the phrase "patterning a shotgun" means standing 30 yards from a target, squeezing the trigger and determining how many pellets put tiny holes in the paper. However, if this is the way you pattern your shotgun, you may be missing more turkey than you're bagging.

First of all, one shot at one distance does not yield enough information. To effectively pattern your shotgun, put targets at 10, 20, 30, 40 and 50 yards. Then you'll be able to determine what your gun does at various distances.

Of course, some sportsmen miss turkey at close range—especially if they're shooting a tight patterning shotgun—because the pattern doesn't have a chance to open up very much from the time it leaves the barrel until the time it contacts the turkey's head and neck. In other words, if the hunter even slightly misses his aim when the turkey is in close, all the pellets in the shell may miss the bird. However, if the turkey is farther away, the pattern opens up and the pellets distribute over a larger region.

Shoot at your targets from the same position you expect to shoot at a gobbler. For most of us, that will be sitting with our back against a tree and the gun up on one knee.

Deciding On Shot Size

What size shot is best for taking turkey? This question is asked and answered every season by every hunter. Everyone has his own opinion, most of which are valid. There's also the philosophy that the gun, not the hunter, dictates what size shot should be used.

Your shotgun patterns every shot size differently. For instance, your shotgun may hold a tight pattern with No. 4s, putting six to 10 pellets in the kill zone of a turkey head target. That same shotgun may throw No. 6 shot all over the paper and only place one or two pellets in the kill zone.

Some shotguns hold a close, tight pattern when shooting Duplex shells, others don't. Some Duplex shells are a combination of No. 2s and No. 4s, while others combine No. 4s and No. 6s. Some shotguns will pattern a specific type of Duplex shell very well, and another type not well at all. The best way to determine which size shot patterns best in each of your guns is to shoot a variety of shot at different distances. Regardless of what shoots best for your partner, get out to a pattern board.

Up to this point patterning your shotgun has been simple. But there is one other factor that plays a major role in the effectiveness of the shell you shoot: the brand name of the particular shell.

By shooting at a pattern board, you can determine how many pellets penetrate the turkey head and neck. Practice from a variety of distances, from 10 to 50 yards. From this information you can determine the effective range of your gun.

You'll find no endorsement of one brand in this book. Instead, remember this: *different brands pattern differently from the same gun.*

A Winchester three-inch magnum, No. 4 shot, for instance, may hold a very tight pattern at 30 yards. But a Remington three-inch magnum, No. 4 shot may produce a very loose pattern. Change shotguns and shoot the two loads again. The results will be different.

To determine which shell and which shot produces the best pattern in your gun, buy several brands of shotgun shells in the same shot size. Test each brand at 10, 20, 30, 40 and 50 yards. If you're not happy with the results, move on to another shot size and repeat the test.

Lovett Williams, one of the nation's leading turkey authorities and wildlife biologists says, "No. 7½s or No. 8s are best for taking turkeys. The turkey's brain and spinal column are very small. To bring a gobbler down, even a small amount of lead that crashes into the spinal column or brain can inflict a mortal wound. Therefore, the more lead the hunter has traveling toward the target area, the greater his chances are for bringing down a tom."

7

Other
Hunting Tools

L uckily, the Good Lord didn't stamp us all out of the same mold. Each of us has our own personality, and each of us has our own preferences. Although the majority of hunters favor a shotgun for turkey hunting, some people favor less popular tools.

Bow And Arrow

The ultimate challenge for many hunters is to take a wary tom with a bow and arrow. The bowhunter puts all of the odds in the gobbler's favor. To compensate he ...

... must be a proficient woodsman because once he locates the turkey, he must determine where he can set up a stand where the turkey will naturally want to go.

... must be able to have a blind that will hide his movements as he draws the bow and still provide an opening through which he can shoot.

... must be able to hold his shot until the gobbler is exactly in the right position so that when he lets the arrow fly, the bird won't jump the string.

... must be able to track and recover the turkey after it is hit.

To bag a turkey with a bow, the hunter needs a fast, flat shooting bow. Like a deer, a turkey can jump the string. The bowhunter should also use an arrow stopper behind his broadhead. This will keep the arrow in the bird once the hit is made.

A string tracker is also helpful, since a gobbler will often run or fly after he's hit. Rarely will a turkey go down immediately. Even if the string tracker breaks, it will lay down a course that a hunter can follow to find his bird.

One technique to take a gobbler with a bow is to build a blind close to a feeder. Cut shooting ports in the blind that can be opened and closed. Once the turkey becomes accustomed to the blind, simply slip inside well before feeding time.

There is, however, the question of whether taking a turkey over a feeder is sportsmanlike. As I view this sport, the person who shoots a turkey over bait is equivalent to the bass fisherman who catches fish with a hand grenade. Sure, he has the trophy, but there's been no sport involved.

A decoy can be used to keep the turkey's attention away from the bowhunter. This should give the bowhunter a chance for an undetected draw. When using a decoy, face it in the opposite direction from which you expect the gobbler. When a tom comes in to a hen decoy, his first move will be to make eye contact. If the decoy is facing away from him, he will probably move in closer to the hen, and the waiting bowhunter.

Crossbow

In some places, hunting with a crossbow is a controversial sport. While some states recognize them as legal tools for harvesting game, others don't. One thing, however, is for sure: Crossbows are accurate, effective tools for harvesting turkey. As with any bowhunter, a string tracker and an arrow stopper are required equipment.

Muzzleloader

Muzzleloading for turkey is usually done by a shotgunner who wants to complicate or improve the sport. The muzzleloader can determine the powder charge, the shot size and the amount of shot that he uses to take the turkey. He can even play with his own homemade duplex load.

But the real skill of muzzleloading is developed by spending time on the pattern board. Generally, the black powder shooter must have the turkey closer than 40 yards. Muzzleloaders must also contend with the fact that since there's a slight delay from the time the percussion cap hits to when the gun fires, the turkey may be spooked.

There is, however, something romantic about bagging a tom

Hunting with a muzzleloader recalls the way our forefathers took wily gobblers when they first reached North America.

with a muzzleloader. It's a type of hunting that's traditional and recalls the way our forefathers took wily gobblers when they first reached North America.

Rifle

Out West, the traditional firearm is a rifle. The land is open country and the shots are long. Some hunters are very sophisticated rifle hunters and use the lighter calibers—like the .222 Rem. and the .243 Win.—for turkey hunting. Generally, these rifles are topped with a 3x9 or 4x10 scope. Shots from 100 to 150 yards are typical for the Western turkey hunter.

Rifle/Shotgun Combos

A firearm that features both a rifle and shotgun offers many turkey hunters the best of both worlds. The shotgun can be used for close shots, while the rifle can reach out for the stubborn gobbler that stays just out of shotgun range.

One drawback with a rifle/shotgun combo is that the hunter has just one shot with each barrel before he must reload.

8

Calling Tools

The human voice was probably the first device ever used to call a wild turkey. Even today, there are proficient turkey callers who use nothing but their voices to call gobblers.

Ben Rodgers Lee, one of North America's leading turkey callers and call manufacturers, used his voice when hunting gobblers long before he started crafting turkey calls. Asked why he started making turkey calls if he was just as effective with his voice, Lee responded, "Well, there are two reasons: First, I consider myself one of a small number of people who can successfully call a turkey with my voice. Second, I can't sell my voice, but I can sell turkey calls."

Just about anything that squeaks, squawks or cries can and will call a wild turkey. Of course, there are some calls that are more effective than others. Obviously, the hunter who masters the diaphragm or slate call has a better chance of killing a turkey than a fellow who rubs two sticks together until they squeak.

Box Call

Some of the first calls ever made were cedar box calls. For instance, M.L. Lynch, founder of the M.L. Lynch Call Company developed a box call in the early 1900s. At that time, box calls were generally whittled out of cedar. The main problem with this type of call was that making two box calls that sounded the same was difficult. If a hunter owned a fine box call, he knew he might never find another just like it.

The hollowed-out box usually had some type of paddle that slid across the top and made clucks, whines, yelps and squeaks. However, in these early models, the lids—or paddles—were rarely of the same thickness or density. Also, the thickness of the walls of the box varied greatly, as did the bottom of the call. Therefore, once a turkey hunter found a box call that made just the right sound, it became a well-guarded treasure.

When Lynch began to work with box calls, he thought of the problems and frustrations he had with them. Then he made a breakthrough that changed the way all box calls were crafted. Mr. Lynch realized there had to be some kind of uniformity in the lid, walls and bottom of the call. So instead of taking one piece of wood and carving out the center, he planed down individual pieces of wood until they were the same thickness. When he had these parts planed to the proper density, he glued each box together. Although this sounds simple, it was revolutionary. In doing so, Lynch not only worked out a method of making all box calls sound alike, he also developed a technique that allowed him to mass produce calls that were easy to use.

Mouth Diaphragm Call

In the late 1920s, another hunter named Jim Radcliff, Sr., was bitten by a mad dog in Mobile, Alabama. This event would not warrant space in this book, except that Radcliff was an avid turkey hunter. So while in New Orleans receiving daily injections for rabies, Radcliff had time on his hands and nothing to do. He visited Bourbon Street. In the French Quarters he found something that helped revolutionize the sport of turkey hunting.

Noticing a man standing on the corner with a small tin cup in front of him, Radcliff listened closely as the entertainer made some of the most beautiful bird calls Radcliff had ever heard. Fascinated by this man's ability to warble out the sounds of feathered creatures, Radcliff continued to watch and listen as the man made various bird calls.

When Radcliff asked the musician if he could make the sound of a wild hen turkey, the street performer had to answer no, although he could imitate a mockingbird, redbird, crow, warbler, sparrow and almost any other bird known to man. So Radcliff went to his hotel and returned with one of his box calls. After listening

With a box call like Lynch's World Champion the experienced turkey caller can produce hen and gobbler sounds.

Mouth diaphragm calls are available with different thicknesses of latex rubber. The call on the left is a single split reed, and the call on the right is a double reed.

to Radcliff's calling on the box, the man decided he probably could imitate a hen turkey.

The bird caller, who had been using a mouth diaphragm, returned to his room and fashioned a mouth call to sound like a hen turkey. After practicing for two or three days, the musician played those sounds for Radcliff on a device made of lead, prophylactic rubber and cloth tape. The sound was so pure that Radcliff had to have one. The street performer taught Radcliff how to use the call and how to make his own diaphragm calls.

From this humble beginning evolved several generations of mouth diaphragm calls, including the single reed, double reed, triple reed, split reed and stack call.

Slate Call

Exactly who invented the slate call is unclear. However, it might have been some youngster who scratched a stick on his slate board while doing his homework. Recognizing that the sound the slate made was much like a hen turkey, he may have dropped his slate board and broke it on purpose. Cupping a piece of slate in his

When using a slate call, slide the peg across the slate to imitate the sounds of a hen turkey.

hand and using a wooden peg, perhaps he discovered what an excellent sound chamber his hand made when he scratched the peg across the slate.

From that primitive beginning, the slate call has changed drastically. M.L. Lynch developed a method of putting a slate on top of a hollow box that could be held in the hand. Using a small peg for a striker, the Lynch Jet was born. It was one of the first commercial slates.

Then in the late 1970s, Lewis Stowe of Gastonia, North Carolina, brought to the market a round slate that fit easily in the hunter's hand and replaced the wood with a plastic sound chamber.

The next evolutionary step in slate calls was the plexiglass slate call where the slate was replaced with a piece of plexiglass and the hunter used either a plexiglass or wood striker. Next came the double slate calls fashioned from plastic or slate. A second piece of

Tube calls like this one from Knight and Hale are a modern version of the old snuff can call.

either plexiglass or slate was situated lower in the sound chamber.

Tube Call

Another turkey call that is relatively new but growing in popularity is the tube call. The tube call was developed from a modified snuff can call. In years past, hunters cut the lid of a snuff can in half and stretched a piece of rubber over the opening in the snuff can. Then by blowing air over the rubber and metering that air the hunter could make the sounds of a wild turkey. With the snuff can call, a hunter could generate sounds that were louder than either the box or diaphragm call. In recent years, call manufacturers like Harold Knight and David Hale, of Knight and Hale Game Calls, have replaced the snuff can with a plastic tube for a modern-day tube call.

Wingbone Call

Another old call that has been modified is the wingbone call, which was built by gluing together three different bones from a turkey's wing to make a small pipe-like call. Most turkey calls operate by blowing air through or over the call. With the wingbone call, however, the sound is made by sucking in rather than blowing. Penn Woods has developed a pipe-like call that is fashioned much like the wingbone call. However, it is made of plastic rather than from the wingbones of a turkey.

The pushbutton call is one of the simplest calls for a hunter to use. Simply hold the box in one hand and push or pull the extruding dowel with the other.

Pushbutton Call

In the early 1940s, 1950s and 1960s, the ability to call the wild turkey was thought to be a gift, bestowed on only the wiliest hunter with the best musical ear. Of those who possessed the gift, one would explain that, ''A caller must spend hours in the woods listening to turkey and then practice for years before sounding like a hen turkey. Most folks don't live long enough or hunt hard enough to master the art of turkey hunting. Why if I hadn't started learning how to call gobblers right after I crawled out of the crib, I wouldn't be able to call a single turkey.''

But in the last few years, the mystique of calling the wild turkey has waned—especially with the new innovations in turkey calls. The pushbutton call, for instance, is a little box with a peg sticking up from its bottom. On top of the box is a small paddle suspended by a round dowel. The hunter holds the box call in his hand and either pushes or pulls the dowel so that the paddle passes over the peg. The resulting sound imitates a hen turkey. The hunter can cut, cackle, purr or yelp the same as he can on any other call. A pushbutton call is easy to use and it brings in many bronze barons each season.

Selecting A Call

The mouth diaphragm call is believed by many to be the ultimate call, because it leaves the hunter's hands free to shoot. Most hunters cup a hand and put it next to their mouth when using this call. When a gobbler is in close and the hunter needs more calling to bring the tom into gun range, the mouth diaphragm is hard to beat.

The slate or friction call requires the hunter to move his hands during the process of calling. However, many turkey hunters believe that there is something magical about the slate. In some locations, the quality of the sound produced by this instrument appears to be more seductive than either the mouth diaphragm or the box call.

Matt Morett, a 17-year-old from Pennsylvania, won the World Friction Calling Championship in 1988 using a slate call. In the woods Morett wears a bib-like apron. As Morett explains, ''I put my hands and my call under this bib to cover my hands when I'm calling. Then, even though my hands are moving, the turkey can't see me call. The apron also seems to muffle the sound, which keeps the turkey from pinpointing the sound. I've found that the

Whichever call the hunter selects, practice is the key to success. The proficient turkey caller will be able to bring the gobblers in close.

slate call is much more interesting to the turkey than the sounds made on the diaphragm or box call.''

Another way to hide the hand movement of a hunter using a call is employed by Allen Jenkins, president of the M.L. Lynch Company. Jenkins uses a portable blind.

"By setting up a portable blind, I can work a turkey with my box call, even when he's only 12 steps away,'' Jenkins says. "However, when a gobbler is close enough for me to take, I won't have my call in my hands anyway. One of the real advantages with the box call is that the average hunter doesn't use it as much as he does the mouth diaphragm. Many times I think hunters overcall with the mouth diaphragm. When you're using a box and the turkey is close, most hunters know to put the call down and get that shotgun up.''

The tube call can be used to call turkey that are close, but most of the sportsmen who work a tube call use it primarily to make turkey shock gobble from a long distance away. Be forewarned: a hunter can call so loudly on the tube call that he scares away the tom.

A pushbutton call splits the difference between requiring a lot of hand movement, like the box call, and no hand movement, like the mouth call. The hunter can hold the pushbutton call with the same hand that holds the forearm of his shotgun. By simply moving his index finger, he can give a light cluck or yelp and bring an old bird to within gun range.

Hunters who get into a discussion as to which call is best must first decide what "best" is. You will want to rank the calls based on how easy they are to use. Almost every call has the ability to bring in a turkey. The important question is: Can *you* use it? The pushbutton, for many people, is the easiest to call a turkey with. The box call is next, with the slate call, wingbone call, mouth diaphragm and tube call becoming more difficult. If possible, carry a variety of calls. Before the day is over, you may have to use every call in your arsenal to lure the gobbler into your sights.

9

Calling Techniques

Wild turkey have their own vocabulary. Scientists and writers attempt to explain the vocabulary of the wild turkey, but their statements and conclusions are often contradictory. Not until someone teaches a turkey to speak English will we find out exactly what each sound means.

Understanding the language of the wild turkey is further complicated by well-intentioned writers and hunters who refer to sounds by different names. For instance, the cutting sound of a hen is described by some people as a series of fast *cuts*, while others call it a series of fast *clucks* or the beginning of a *cackle*. Here's a simple, straightforward explanation of the sounds turkey make.

Hen Calls

Hens have a wide vocabulary, and their calls mean different things at specific times of the year. The emotion or feeling of the hen when she's making a call helps to explain the call and allows the hunter to know what she's trying to say.

Cluck. Hen turkey cluck like chickens. Often a hen will cluck before she flies down off the roost or when she's feeding. She'll give excited clucks when she's ready to mate or looking for a gobbler. And she'll cluck loudly to let her poults know her location. Sometimes she'll give a contented cluck, much like a person who hums when busy with an enjoyable project. She'll also cluck to let a gobbler know her location. By the tone of her cluck, she can express desire or contentedness.

Yelp. The yelp, which is the second most common call given by a hen turkey, has many meanings. The hen yelps to let other turkey know where she is, to call her brood together and to let a gobbler know where to find her. A dominant hen will yelp to express her dominance over other hens in the flock. And sometimes hens seem to yelp just to be social.

Cackle. This is an excited call. Listen for the cackle when the hen flies down from the roost, flies over a fence or is excited about mating.

Cut. Cutting is when a hen gives several clucks in rapid succession, making this one of the most exciting mating calls a hen can give to the gobbler. When a hen starts cutting to a gobbler, mating is near.

Assembly Call Of The Old Hen. This call is given by the matriarch of the flock and is primarily heard in the fall when the flock is scattered. At that time, the flock's primary concern is to get back together. So the old hen starts off with a series of loud yelps that builds to a crescendo and then dies away and stops completely. The assembly call of the old hen means that she is at a place where the other birds should flock together. This is one of the primary calls that the hunter uses to take turkey in the fall.

Purr. This is a low, guttural sound a hen makes when she's feeding.

Putt. This alarm call of the wild turkey can be given by both the gobbler and the hen—usually just before the turkey plans to run off. When a turkey starts putting, a hunter can rest assured that his hunt is over.

Tree Call. The tree call is a light, soft series of yelps that can barely be heard. The tree call is given at first light by the hens while they're still on the roost. Many times the gobbler will answer a tree call.

Gobbler Calls

Gobble. When a turkey gobbles, he's telling the hens where he's located and that he wants them to come to him to be bred. He's also exerting his dominance. Usually when a boss or a dominant tom gobbles, the subordinate gobblers in the area will quit gobbling. Since he's the dominant bird, he claims the right to breed all the hens and seems to be reminding the subordinate toms to stay clear.

A gobble can also be a challenge to other toms. It's almost an open invitation to a battle of spurs, beaks and wings.

Young Gobbler's Squealing Call. Often called the kee-kee run, this call is made by a young gobbler before his voice is fully developed. A bird making a kee-kee run sounds much like a teenage boy whose voice cracks. Sometimes he talks low like a man and at other times high like a boy. A young gobbler's squealing call, which is usually a high-pitched whistle followed by a series of coarse yelps, is effective in the fall. This call is the one young gobblers often use to find their mothers or locate each other.

Gobbler Yelp. Often, especially in the fall, gobblers will give a coarse yelp that is heard when there is a flock traveling together. The gobbler yelp is generally used by the birds to locate each other. However, this call can also be heard in the spring.

Cluck. When a gobbler comes in to meet a hen, sometimes he will come in clucking to let the hen know his location.

Putt. When a gobbler putts, the hunt is over. The putt means that he's preparing to shift into high gear and leave the area. When you hear a turkey putt, get ready to shoot or change locations.

Drum. If you've ever heard an 18-wheel truck tackle a steep grade and shift gears, then you know what a turkey's drumming sounds like. Drumming is a low, quiet sound gobblers make to let hens know their location. Many times when a turkey is coming to your call, you will hear the drumming sound long before you see the turkey. Turkey most often drum when they strut, and the drumming sound usually will be heard along with the sound of the turkey's wing tips dragging across the leaves and dirt.

How And When To Use Hen Calls

"When I turkey hunt, I cluck three times and then throw my turkey call away," one old timer told me. "I'm convinced that the reason more hunters don't take more turkey is that they call too much. If you hear a turkey gobble, cluck three times. He will gobble back. That old tom will know your position. Sooner or later he'll come to you. If you keep making calls, you'll mess up. Patience will kill more gobblers than calling."

That advice was given to me many years ago, and I've often thought about the wisdom contained in the old man's words when I've caught myself overcalling.

Cluck. A simple cluck is as effective as any call that can be made. It's also one of the easiest calls to make. On a mouth diaphragm, meter a small burst of air over your tongue and past the

When a gobbler comes in to meet a hen, light clucking with a box call may be all that is required to bring him into your effective range.

diaphragm. On a box call, simply make one short, quick note. You can even rest your thumbs on the top of the box and tap the lid to make a cluck. When using the slate call, give a short strike across the slate to create a single note. And on the pushbutton call, gently tap the dowel to produce a cluck. The cluck is especially effective when a gobbler is in close range and you don't need to do much calling.

Yelp. The yelp is the call that hunters use most of the time. Follow a cluck with some light yelping, because a cluck may be misinterpreted by a gobbler as an alarm putt. If a cluck is followed by a series of yelps, there's no way a tom can misinterpret the call for a putt.

The faster the yelps are given, the more excited the hen appears to be. The louder the yelps, generally, the more pleading the call. You can put many levels of emotion into a series of yelps. To produce a yelp on a mouth diaphragm meter the air in short bursts over the tongue and between the tongue and diaphragm. With a slate or plexiglass friction call, move the peg in a circle. The faster you move the peg, the more excited the yelps sound. With the box call, move the paddle across the edge of the box in a regular cadence. With the pushbutton call, push the dial on the call back and forth with a regular rhythm to imitate the yelp. The yelp is often given when you want to call the bird in without getting him too excited.

Cackle. The cackle is a series of fast yelps and denotes excitement in the hen. If a gobbler is slow to come in, use the cackle to speed up the bird's progress and excite him with the prospect of mating. To produce the cackle with the mouth diaphragm, blow quickly, using the tongue to pick out each note of the cackle on the rubber membrane of the call. On the box call, quickly move the lid of the box over the side of the call in rapid succession. On the slate call, make the same circles as when giving the yelp but make them quicker, putting excitement into the cackle. With a pushbutton call, quickly push or pull the dowel to imitate the cackle.

Assembly Call. This call is primarily given in the fall and consists of a series of loud yelps with a lot of pleading. The same technique we described when talking about the yelp call applies to the assembly yelp, except that you should start the call off quietly and build each yelp louder and louder. The assembly call is the vocalization that the hen uses when she's gathering her flock.

Purr. This very subtle, contented call often is used by a hen

To turn a gobbler, many hunters will "throw" their call to one side. With a mouth diaphragm this is accomplished with a cupped hand which will deflect the sound in the desired direction.

when she's feeding and is especially effective for a hunter to use when a gobbler hangs up just out of gun range. This call tells the gobbler that although he's close by and strutting his stuff, the hen could care less. Oftentimes, this call will hurt an old bird's pride so badly that he will come waltzing right in.

The purr is produced very softly on a diaphragm call with only the smallest bit of air forced between the tongue and the diaphragm. On the slate call, drag the peg across the slate with the slightest pressure. On a box, move the lid lightly across the side of the box.

Putt. The only time you should use the putt is when a gobbler comes strutting in and you want to break him out of the strut. The putt is a sharp, loud cluck. This call will successfully break a turkey out of his strut. Usually a tom will stick his head straight up when he hears that call. You then have only a second to shoot. The only difference between the cluck and the putt is the severity and the crispness of the sound. The cluck is a soft sound; the putt is a very hard sound. Rarely should you use this call.

Tree Call. To make a tree call, use the same action described to give a yelp, but reduce the amount of air being forced through the diaphragm call. This produces a lighter yelp. With friction calls, use less force on the lid of the box. With a slate call, use less force on the striker. On the pushbutton call, pull the dowel much easier and slower.

The putt call should only be used to break a gobbler out of his strut. Usually, the tom will stick his head straight up. The hunter will then have only a second to shoot.

The tree call is given first thing in the morning before first light when the turkey are beginning to wake up. The tree call lets the gobbler know the "hen's" location—just in case he's in the mood when he flies down.

How And When To Use Gobbler Calls

Gobbler calls are the most dangerous to employ, because these are the sounds that attract other hunters. Be careful!

Gobble. Several box and tube calls are available that will make the gobble. The gobble is most often produced by shaking the call. Here's what to remember:

1) Have your back against a tree and watch for other hunters before you gobble.

2) Realize that if you gobble there's a good chance that you may run off the turkey you're trying to call. If the tom is not the dominant gobbler, he may leave rather than come into what he believes will be a fight. However, if the turkey is a dominant bird, the tom may think that another gobbler has moved into his territory and come in ready to fight.

3) Use the gobble call as a last resort.

Young Gobbler's Squealing Call. The squeal is usually three high-pitched calls followed by a series of yelps. You can make it on the diaphragm call by pushing your tongue into the diaphragm so that the rubber is stretched to give the high squeal. Then loosen the pressure on the diaphragm to give a series of yelps. A young gobbler's squealing call can be productive during the fall after the turkey have scattered. Sometimes this call is successful in the spring.

Yelp. The gobbler's yelp, which is seldom heard, is a coarse form of yelping. Generally, the yelp will be made by young gobblers. To make this sound, most hunters prefer using a coarser box call or the opposite side that produces hen calls. A triple reed or split reed diaphragm call will also work. The gobbler yelp often will bring a gobbler to the gun during the fall and winter months when large flocks roam together.

Cluck. The cluck is a good call to use in the fall. Usually the gobbler cluck is more coarse and deeper than the hen cluck.

Putt. Already described under hen calls, the only time to use the tom putt is when you are attempting to break a gobbler out of a strut.

Drum. This call is made by the turkey and rarely, if ever, is made by a hunter.

Calling Scenario

The best way to approach the use of calls is to understand that a turkey hunt is like a chess game as described in the introduction of this book. Although there are certain moves that the players learn to play the game, the real masters of the sport often break the rules to produce better results. Here's several standard plays in general calling situations.

Scenario One. You go into the woods a little before daylight and hear a turkey gobble. You slip into an area where you can see 30 to 40 yards in all directions, and face the direction you expect the turkey to come from. You give a soft tree call. The turkey gobbles back.

In a few minutes, you hear the turkey fly down from the roost and gobble as he hits the ground. Now you give a few light yelps. The tom gobbles again and moves closer. In a matter of minutes, the turkey appears and walks straight toward you. Your shotgun rests on your knee and is pointed at the turkey. When the bird is at 30 yards, you squeeze the trigger. Bang! The hunt is over.

Scenario Two. You hear the turkey fly down from the roost and gobble as he hits the ground. You give a few light yelps. The tom gobbles back but doesn't move closer. Although you cluck and yelp, the bird keeps his distance. You begin cutting to the bird. Hearing the call, the turkey comes in. Bang! The hunt is over.

Scenario Three. The gobbler flies down from the roost, gobbles and moves toward you. Then he stops just 50 yards away, strutting and drumming but not coming close enough for a shot. You make some soft clucks. Although the tom moves closer, he stops again at 40 yards, again strutting, drumming and refusing to come closer. You give some light purrs that sound like a contented hen. The turkey moves closer. Bang! The hunt is over.

Scenario Four. The gobbler flies down and comes in but hangs up at 50 yards. Although you try all the tactics in Scenario Three, none work. Using the mouth diaphragm call, you direct your call to a tree 10 yards behind you. The tom thinks the hen is walking away from him and moves closer. Bang! The hunt is over.

Scenario Five. Same situation. You use all the above tactics but none work. The gobbler is still hung up at 50 yards and refuses to move. You let the tom walk off. When the bird is well out of sight, you circle to the right of the bird, take another stand, change calls and try again. This time the gobbler walks right in. Bang! The hunt is over.

Scenario Six. The tom flies down, gobbles and walks away.

You follow the turkey and call occasionally—sometimes yelping loudly. Finally, the gobbler stops and comes back to you. Bang! The hunt is over.

Scenario Seven. The turkey gobbles from the roost, but because he's in an area where he's been hunted heavily, he won't come to any call at first light. You leave the woods, return to the area around 10:00 a.m. and take a stand. You give some light clucks and yelps. The turkey comes to you silently, never gobbling. Bang! The hunt is over.

These are just a few of the scenarios that may occur when a hunter takes his calls and goes into the woods to pit his skills against the master of the woods. Although knowing when to call and what calls to give is important, understanding where a turkey wants to go and why will result in more birds being bagged.

Also important to successfully bagging gobblers is learning when not to call and how not to overcall. Put bluntly, one of the biggest problems novice turkey hunters face is knowing when to shut up. Turkey calls were designed to make gobblers come to turkey hunters, not to be used as conversational tools to allow sportsmen to continuously talk to birds. As soon as a hunter determines that a tom is moving toward him, the most effective call he can use is no call at all.

One of the best ways to learn to talk turkey and to begin to understand the language that hunters use to communicate with wily gobblers is to attend a turkey calling contest. At a contest, not only will you get to hear master woodsmen give the sounds and calls of the wild turkey, but you'll also have an opportunity to talk to these hunters and learn when they use the calls and why.

Often contestants are willing and eager to share their turkey calling knowledge with beginners. Sometimes call manufacturers will be in attendance to show their products and help hunters learn how to call.

Another way to learn how to talk like a turkey is through turkey hunting videos and tapes. Almost every call manufacturer produces some type of turkey hunting video cassette tape. By using a cassette, the hunter can hear and see an expert give a call, and then he can imitate the call. By recording the call you make and then listening to the difference between your call and the call made by the man on the cassette, you'll be able to hear how close you are coming to imitating the call you need to make.

Turkey hunting videos for the most part show the hunter how, where, when and why to use a specific call. Many of the videos on

Knowing when to call and when to keep quiet is often the difference between winning and losing the game of turkey hunting.

By sitting directly behind the shooter the caller views the gobbler from the hunter's perspective. He can then adjust his calling to bring the turkey to the spot where the shooter has a clear, killing shot.

the market present the information as though the viewer is on a turkey hunt, allowing him to see a master hunter set up and call a turkey to within gun range. This is probably the best way to simulate a successful hunt.

Yet another way to learn how to hunt and call the wild turkey is to read books about turkey hunting. Reading gives you the chance to learn from the best hunters and callers in North America. It gives you access to more information than could ever be crammed into a video tape.

10

Calling Situations

No one can draw up *the* blueprint to outfox the wily wild turkey. But in certain calling situations, there are proven techniques that you can employ to increase your chances for success.

Flat Terrain

A hunter who locates a gobbler in flat, open terrain has three options:

1) He can get the turkey excited on the roost by cutting and cackling. Then, when the gobbler flies down, the bird will run in so fired up that he never stops to consider why he can't see the hen.

2) He can call very little, directing his calls in several directions. The gobbler won't know the hen's exact location. Even though the tom may move in slower, he will come in because he's yet to pinpoint the source of the calling.

3) The hunter directs his calls as far behind him as he can. The tom, assuming that the hen is much farther away, will be less careful when he gets within gun range.

Dense Brush

As a general rule, turkey will not walk through dense cover. Yes, there are some birds in every flock that will break this rule, but that is so infrequent that your best bet is to avoid thick cover.

Here's why: After the turkey poult climbs out of his egg, his mother teaches him that everything in the woods that he doesn't recognize will eat him. Hawks and owls swoop down from above. Coyote, bobcats, foxes and wild dogs jump out from behind bushes. And hunters hide in thick places to shoot turkey.

Therefore, a turkey learns at a very early age that anything he can't recognize is dangerous and that any thick cover holds a predator. If you set up in heavily wooded cover, you'll be sitting there for some time before you ever spot a turkey.

When hunting areas with a large amount of undergrowth search for the places where a turkey naturally walks and feeds. Locate a clear spot in the woods, then sit down and start your calling.

Rain And Snow

One of the best ways to take a gobbler during the spring is to hunt during a rainstorm. The turkey won't be able to hear your approach and he's not as likely to see your movement since the rain is bouncing off the leaves, bushes and trees. More than likely, that tom has never before encountered a hunter during a rainstorm. The result is that he may not be as wary on rainy days as he is on clear, bluebird days.

One of the finest gobblers I ever took was bagged in a driving rainstorm. Although the bird was in the middle of a clear pasture with several hens, a friend and I called to the tom and he immediately fired back a gobble and slowly walked over to the edge of the field. He had an eight-inch beard, three-quarter-inch spurs and weighed 19½ pounds.

Early Season Gobblers

The term "early season gobblers" means different things in various parts of the country. In states where there is a one-week turkey season there's neither an early nor a late season. There's only, "the season." In other states the season begins around March 15 and runs until the end of April. Often the toms won't be gobbling during the first part of the season.

Therefore, let's define "early season" as the time of the year just prior to the mating season. Although toms may be gobbling, they probably have not set up their territories or bred any hens. This early season may be the most difficult time of the year to call and bag a longbeard. The juvenile males, which are commonly referred to as jakes, will come to hen calls. But the older toms are usually reluctant to gobble.

So during the early part of the season, woodsmanship plays a

For someone unaccustomed to hunting at high altitudes, conditioning plays a major role in the hunter's ability to perform during the hunt.

One of the best ways to call a stubborn gobbler is to hunt him during a rainstorm.

greater role in the turkey hunter's success than his ability to call a turkey. By using the term, ''woodsmanship,'' we're referring to the hunter's knowledge of the woods and the turkey he's hunting. A successful turkey hunter with woodsmanship skills can consistently bag a gobbler without using a call. This type of hunter learns everything he can about gobblers by watching where they roost and strut, and what fields they like to frequent. Generally, this turkey chaser will also know where a specific turkey is at throughout the day. Therefore, when the time comes for him to take that turkey, he simply sets up an ambush along the route the gobbler normally travels.

When a tom is not gobbling in the early season, determining his roost tree, strutting grounds and feeding sites can mean the difference between success and failure.

Late Season Gobblers
After the hens have started to go to their nests, hunting late in the morning may be the most productive time. Late in the season, a hen will usually meet her gobbler as soon as he flies down off the roost. She will remain with him for an hour or two after daylight, and by 9:00 or 10:00 a.m. will slip away to return to her nest.

To successfully hunt a gobbler, we must realize what's driving his actions. When the tom lifts out of the tree in the morning and has all those beautiful hens just waiting for his services, he feels as though he's the most desirable male in the world. He gets all puffed up, struts his feathers and believes he's a great lover.

But in the late season, come mid-morning, this "world's greatest lover" finds himself alone. Not only does he not have a hen to mate, he doesn't have any company. He's by himself and brokenhearted. By that time of the morning, a gobbler is generally willing to talk to and pay a visit to any hen in the woods. So if you are in the woods when the tom is in that frame of mind, there's a good chance you can carry a tom home.

The Late, Late Season

The late, late season is when the hens are on the nest and care less about the gobblers. However, toms are holding out hope for an opportunity to breed one more hen. By this time most gobblers have been well-educated by hunters. So at the first sound of a hunter's aggressive call the gobbler may walk off without ever making a sound.

However, if the turkey hears some soft clucks, yelps and purrs like a contented hen that has decided to be bred one more time, he may go quickly to her. Usually, gobblers in the late, late season will not respond to any type of calling. That means the hunter must once again rely on his woodsmanship to set up along the route that the bird normally follows every day.

River Bottom Swamps

When I'm hunting river bottom swamps I begin the day with the understanding that I will get wet. So I carry with me a boot dryer, extra boots and several sets of camouflage. I assume that I will either wade a creek, fall in a mud hole or get rained on during my stay.

Sometimes, you'll hear a turkey gobble on the other side of the slough or creek. Although some hunters may have called a bird across water, it doesn't happen often. The best technique to take a turkey that's across the water from you is to wade the water and get on the same side as the bird. Turkey will wade in water that's not too deep, but they generally prefer not to. The easier you can make the route from where he is to where you are, the more likely you are to bag the bird.

Three other factors that contribute to the swamp hunter's success or failure are mosquitoes, ticks and redbugs. Each of these has the potential to make a man with a will of steel flinch, squint or move when a turkey is looking at him. Even when the tom is standing at 30 yards and the hunter is looking down the barrel of the shotgun with the bead superimposed on the bird's neck, a mosquito buzzing in the hunter's ear or a tick crawling up his back can break his concentration.

The simplest solution to this problem is to use 100 percent deet insect repellent. But remember that the insect repellent you put on before daylight may have washed off after you waded the first stretch of flooded timber. So carry insect repellent with you at all times, and reapply it after you come out of the water.

The good news about hunting swamp turkey is that the hunter can move more quietly through the water than the woods. So he may move even closer to the bird before he begins to call.

Deserts

In areas where turkey have a vast amount of green grasses and shrubs, a large percentage of the water they need comes from the vegetation they eat. However, in dry, arid regions like the desert country in parts of the West, the only source of water that the turkey have is stock tanks and ponds. Since water is just as critical for the birds to survive as food, setting up around stock tanks and ponds is an excellent way to locate and harvest desert turkey.

Something else that is important to desert turkey is shade. When desert birds are not eating or drinking, they're usually staying in the shade. Hunt around food, water and shade, or around the routes a tom will travel to reach these places.

Desert turkey hunters also learn that Rio Grande turkey have two gears: stop and trot. Eastern birds walk from place to place and will fly or run only when alarmed. But the Rio Grande desert birds either sit tight or trot to reach a certain spot. Therefore, when you hear a Rio Grande turkey that's not around food, water or shade gobble, he may be half a mile away before you hear him again.

The sound of a gobble carries much farther in the desert than in mountainous areas and the woods of the East. Although a tom may gobble a half mile away, he may sound as close as 100 yards away. On the Harrison Ranch near Sonora, Texas, hunters often hear 40-50 toms gobbling in one morning. However, many of these gobblers are a mile or more away.

Another critical factor in successfully hunting desert turkey is the hunter's ability to find a place from which to call. When a turkey gobbles in the East, the hunter can usually sit down next to a tree that's wider than his shoulders and be well camouflaged.

Merriams will respond to calling much more readily than eastern turkey. But hunting in the mountains is not an easy task for the flatlander.

However, on the desert where there are few trees, locating anything high enough to hide behind can be tough.

One Rio Grande turkey I took in Texas was called up to an abandoned calf feeder. The feeder was between the turkey and a stock tank, and it was the only vertical relief for about one-quarter mile in all directions. If you are accustomed to hunting eastern turkey, you will soon discover that there is much to learn about hunting western turkey.

However, desert turkey may come to calling easier than eastern birds. Since western hunters traditionally bag gobblers with rifles, many desert turkey have rarely been called.

Western Mountain Turkey

When I hunted Merriam turkey in the Rocky Mountains of New Mexico I learned that I had been lied to all my life. Everyone had said Merriam gobblers were easy to hunt. The Merriam birds did respond to calls much more readily than eastern turkeys. But hunting in the mountains at 8,000 feet above sea level was not an easy task for a flatlander like myself.

I never realized the difference in hunting at high altitudes until I tried to run up a mountain the first morning. After 50 yards, I felt like the biggest gorilla in Africa was sitting on my chest. The muscles in my lungs were screaming for air, despite the fact that I had turkey hunted almost every day for six weeks, walking six to 10 miles per day. Some 30 yards up the mountain, my hunting companion whispered loudly, "Come on John, let's go."

Mountain turkey seem to prefer walking over a mountain rather than down a valley. For someone unaccustomed to hunting at high altitudes, conditioning plays a major role in your ability to perform during the hunt.

11

Pre-Season Scouting

What images come to mind when someone starts talking about scouting for turkey? Most of us probably imagine long walks through the woods looking for tracks, feathers or signs. This is one of the most popular methods, but it's also one of the most time consuming.

Aerial Photos And Topo Maps

A more productive technique is to scout from the air. Your first reaction to this might be, "I neither like airplanes nor do I have the money to rent a plane to look for turkey." But you can do aerial reconnaissance without ever leaving the ground.

The U.S. Geological Survey has aerial photos of most of the land in every state. If you can describe the region you want to hunt, chances are good that they can provide you with an aerial map of the area. If you're serious about your turkey hunting and don't want to waste time, buy aerial photo maps.

When you first study these maps, look for access points to the property you intend to hunt. If roads or right-of-ways are dimly marked, highlight them with a yellow marker. Use a red highlighter to specify power lines and firebreaks, a blue highlighter to denote trails.

An aerial photo is also important when you locate a turkey. Use different colored pens to mark the areas where you find birds.

Finding an area where a gobbler has been strutting and dragging his wings—like this tom is doing—is an excellent place to start your calling.

Then if you strike out on one bird, you can always try another. Besides noting access to the woods, an aerial photo can tell you where the turkey should be. These photos show fields, creek bottoms, pine plantations and clear-cuts.

However, an aerial photo doesn't show you the elevation changes of the area. For this reason, buy a topographic map as well. These are also available from the U.S. Geological Survey. From the information on a topographic map, you'll be able to see the gradients of draws and valleys. In addition to seeing what type of terrain the gobblers will favor, you can see which swamps or cliffs you should avoid.

Once you've studied the maps, divide specific areas where you think the birds should be into two categories, the easy gobblers and the tough toms. The easy gobblers are found close to roads. The tough toms live away from the roads. Your only access to the tough toms might be by walking along creek bottoms or firebreaks. Once you've done as much scouting as you can, take to the woods.

Scouting The Woods

When scouting for turkey, the first place to look for sign is on roads and trails. Search for tracks, droppings and places where gobblers may have strutted.

The second easiest place to look is at the edge of a field. If gobblers are using a field, there should be droppings or tracks around that field. Next, search for feathers. Turkey molt, and always seem to be breaking off and losing feathers. Also, check for places where turkey have been scratching for feed.

On these scouting excursions, go with the expectation that you will find turkey sign. This anticipation is an important key to a successful hunt. If two hunters enter the woods and one hunter says, "I'm going to look for turkey, but I don't think that I'll be able to find any," odds are, he won't. He might look at a spot 200 yards away and think, "I bet a turkey wouldn't use that area, travel that path or feed in that region." So he doesn't investigate. Nor does he find any promising turkey sign.

The other hunter, meanwhile, goes into the woods *expecting* to find turkey. He tells himself: "Although I don't really believe a turkey would use that area, I'll go over there and look just in case." This hunter is more likely to find turkey sign. The attitude and mind-set will determine what you discover.

Once you locate a place that the birds are using, learn all you can about what they are doing. Look for roost trees. These are easy to pick out because there will be lots of turkey droppings underneath. Hunt for strut areas where a gobbler dragged his wings as he strutted. Search for dusting sites where a turkey rolled in the dust to clean his feathers. If you're hunting in the desert, find places where a gobbler may feed, water, strut, loaf, walk or stay in the shade.

Then it's on to the next phase of scouting.

Scouting The Early Morning

The best time to determine where the gobblers are roosting is the early morning. To bag a bird, you'll need to get close to the roost before daylight. Then you can call him, and take him when he flies down from the roost. To find a gobbler's roost tree, however, you'll need to go into the woods before daylight.

Once you're in the woods, listen for the tom to gobble. As

soon as you hear it, take a compass reading on the bird. You've already studied the maps and walked in the woods enough to know the gobblers location. Record where, when and in what direction the turkey gobbled. At least two weeks before the season, find as many gobbling birds as you can and pinpoint them on your aerial photo.

Then, one week before the season opens, learn more about each bird. First move close to each bird while he's still on the roost. Wait for him to fly down. Listen to see which way he goes. Once you're convinced that the bird is out of sight, walk to the roost. Check for any creeks, ditches, thick places, terrain breaks or fences that may prohibit the tom from coming to a possible blind. By knowing which way the bird flies off the roost, you can pick your blind. Once you've compiled this information, you're ready for opening morning.

Hunting Giveaway Gobblers

Giveaway gobblers are those birds that every turkey hunter can hear by standing on the road next to his car. These are the toms that roost within 200 yards of the road. And come opening morning, you can bet that there will be more than just one hunter after each giveaway gobbler. That can be frustrating and dangerous.

Don't bother with giveaway gobblers. Take to the woods, and get into some country that few people take the time to enjoy.

Hunting Strut Zones

It's not uncommon for gobblers to have specific places where they like to strut and meet hens. Each gobbler may have two or three different strut zones, and he'll show up at these places at the same time every day. If you can locate one of these zones, chances are you'll have a good shot at bagging a bird. Here's how:

Once you find a strut zone add that information to your aerial photo. For instance, one of my maps has this information: Bent Road Gobbler struts in the sage field at 9:45 a.m. and along Cross Creek Road at 2:17 p.m. Broken Bridge Tom struts at 8:15 a.m. close to that old broken bridge; at 1:30 p.m. he struts in the pea patch behind the tenant farmer's house.

Then set up a full day of appointments with gobblers. This technique requires some intensive scouting. But scouting can be, and should be, as enjoyable and rewarding as the hunt itself.

12

Locating Gobblers

S couting is the best way to learn where turkey are traveling. But to pinpoint a gobbler, you must talk with the tom. To do that, you can either use a call that will make the turkey shock gobble, or you can use a hen call that may bring the turkey in to you.

Regardless of the call you use, you don't want the bird to pinpoint your position. By using a call other than a hen call, you can keep up with a turkey's movements. Also, by using calls that make a turkey gobble as a reaction rather than gobbling for mating purposes, you can often locate two or three gobblers in one area.

Shock Gobble

Bass fishermen have learned that bass don't have to be hungry to hit a bait. If a fisherman drops a lure close to a bass that is holding tight, the fish will instinctively strike the lure, even though it may not need to eat.

Making a turkey shock gobble is a similar technique. When a hunter causes a tom to shock gobble, the turkey is not gobbling to let a hen know where he is. Rather, he is gobbling in response to a sound.

A shock gobble might be described as what happens when you walk down a dark corridor late at night. If a prankster hides in the shadows and then jumps out, your natural reaction is to jump back and yell. When that sound is made by a gobbler, we call it a shock gobble.

Let's discuss the calls that will make toms shock gobble.

Owl Hoot. During the spring gobbling season, a tom that's spent his night sleeping on a high limb has been dreaming about the beautiful young hens he's going to mate at dawn. Spring is the only season when he gets to mate with hens, so even before the first rays of light crawl across the horizon, the old boy has sex on his mind. His testosterone level is high, and he's ready to talk about mating with the first sound he hears.

One of the sounds that a tom gobbles to in the spring is the hooting of the barred owl, which are common east of the Rocky Mountains. The hunter who can imitate the hoot of a barred owl can locate a turkey in the early hours just before daylight until about 8:00 or 9:00 a.m.

Although there are several ways you can learn to hoot like an owl, the most common method is to practice hooting without a call. It's not difficult to master. The biggest problem is for the hunter to overcome his own fear of sounding stupid. For the more inhibited hunter, there are commercially made owl hooters, some of which will hoot louder than the human voice. Almost all call companies manufacture some type of owl hooter. Long-time favorites include those made by Knight and Hale, Butski and the M.L. Lynch Company.

However, just because the hunter can hoot like an owl doesn't mean he can force a turkey to gobble. Owl hooting has a particular cadence just like turkey calling. There are many variations of owl hooting, but the most popular rhythm sounds like the words, "Who cooks for you, who cooks for you all." Also, owls sometimes give a laugh which is called a chuckle. This chuckle is one long "hoot."

The first call that the hunter should give on an owl hooter is one short, low hoot. If there's a tom close by, he'll gobble. Then you won't blow him off the limb with some loud calling. There's no point in using a cannon to kill a fly if a fly swatter is just as effective. Many times a hunter can spook a bird if he owl hoots too loudly and is too close to the tom. Another reason for giving one short, low hoot is because when toms are active and ready to mate, they'll gobble in the middle of the hoot. If a hunter is making a loud or long hoot, he may never hear the tom gobble.

If, however, the turkey doesn't gobble after one, short, low hoot, make a longer, louder, one note hoot. If the tom still doesn't

One of the sounds that a tom will shock gobble to is the hoot of a barred owl. Most manufacturers offer such a call, as well as an audio cassette to help you learn.

gobble back, then a loud, one note hoot is suggested. Once again, remember the longer and louder the hunter hoots, the less likely he is to hear a turkey gobble if the bird gobbles in the middle of the hooting.

If the tom still doesn't gobble, use a six- to eight-note call like the "Who cooks for you, who cooks for you all," call mentioned earlier. If a gobbler doesn't respond, make a loud owl call and include several chuckles or laughs at the end.

One of the main reasons for hooting loudly is to communicate with other owls that hear the hunter's hooting and hoot back. Actually the owl that's hooting at you may be what causes a turkey to gobble on a distant ridge, even though the tom didn't hear your hooting. On one occasion I hooted from a high ridge, had an owl answer me from a long way off and heard a tom on a distant ridge gobble. I climbed into my vehicle, drove around to the ridge where the turkey gobbled, started hooting again and had the tom shock gobble.

Owl hooting is fun, and such an integral part of turkey hunting that most turkey calling contests include owl hooting.

Crow Call. Turkey will also gobble to a crow call, which is a high-pitched, shrill sound that has the ability to put goose bumps on the back of a human's neck and make a tom gobble even if he doesn't want to. No call will work all the time to make a particular critter do anything. Therefore, a turkey hunter who hopes to be successful will have more than one type of call to make a bird gobble. Since some toms won't answer an owl hooter but may gobble to a crow call, carry both.

There are some outstanding turkey hunters and guides who prefer to use a crow call rather than an owl hooter, because they believe it's more effective. Others like to blow a crow call after about 10:00 a.m. until 3:00 p.m. If the call is used correctly, the hunter will begin to call in crows. Just calling in anything beats no action. But the crow call can make locked-lipped toms talk, especially in the middle of the day.

One of the best ways to learn to call crows is to either hunt with a master turkey hunter who has experience calling, or buy a cassette tape on calling crows. Lohman's produces a fine crow call and tape on crow calling, as does Burnham Brothers. If you can make a gobbler talk with a crow call in the middle of the day, you have a reasonably good chance of bagging that bird.

Hawk Call. The hawk call is the third call that the hunter can use to invoke the shock gobble from the turkey. The call of the

The successful turkey hunter will use more than just one type of call to make a tom shock gobble. An owl, crow and hawk call are the three most popular.

hawk is a high, shrill call that sounds much like a dog whistle. Perhaps the reason the turkey will gobble is because it's such a high, shrill call that it irritates the bird into gobbling.

The hawk call is a good call to use in the middle of the day and should make the tom talk. However, of the calls that a hunter can use to locate a gobbler, the owl hooter may be the most universally accepted and productive.

Other Weird Sounds. Some friends and I were driving down a high, rocky, mountain, dirt road when the four wheel drive vehicle we were in hit a bump, and the springs squealed. At that moment a turkey gobbled on the other side of a pasture. We had been hunting all morning long and had been unable to get close to a gobbler.

We pulled off the road, climbed a mountain and got above the turkey. We started calling. Finally, we took him. Had the car not hit the bump, we'd never have located that gobbler and would have driven right past him.

Turkey hunter Allen Jenkins often tells the story about a turkey called the School Bus Gobbler. Every morning when a school bus went by a certain portion of woods and hit a bump, this bird would gobble. That was the only sound the turkey would gobble to and was the only time of day the bird would talk.

Many NAHC members have probably heard a turkey gobble to the sound of a shotgun discharging. Many old timers say when all else fails to make a turkey gobble, shoot your gun and listen.

Another sound turkey will gobble to is thunder. If you can't locate turkey any other way, go into the woods during a thunderstorm, and listen when the lightning pops and the thunder rolls. You'll usually hear every turkey in the woods gobble.

Toms will also answer car horns as well as the horn of a tugboat on the river. They'll gobble to the loud mooing of a cow or a bridge rattling when a car passes over it. There seems to be many sounds that make a tom gobble. But on some mornings, a tom will keep his mouth shut even if a stick of dynamite goes off under his roost tree.

Put A Gobbler To Bed

One of the best ways to ensure turkey hunting success is to put a gobbler to bed. Go into the woods a little before fly-up time in the late afternoon and listen for a turkey to fly up to the roost. If you can find where a gobbler is roosting, then the next morning before daylight slip into that area and set up within 75-100 yards of

If you can't get a stubborn old tom to shock gobble, visit the woods during a thunderstorm. Then listen after each lightning crack. You'll probably hear every turkey in the woods shock gobble, including that stubborn old tom.

where the tom is roosting. Start calling the bird and you will have a very good chance of bagging that tom.

Another advantage of putting the birds to bed is that if you watch a gobbler fly up to roost, you can pinpoint where the gobbler is roosting, where the hens are roosting and decide where you need to set up to be between them.

One problem associated with putting gobblers to bed is that many hunters are so anxious to get out of the woods before dark that they spook the birds off the roost. Then all of their efforts are meaningless. Remember: If you leave before dark the turkey will see you and be suspicious of any calling. Therefore, the wise hunter will stay until well after sunset so the turkey can't see him crawl out of the woods. By the same token, if you put a gobbler to roost and plan to hunt him the next morning you must reach the place well before first light. The same darkness you used to hide under as you slipped away is also needed to camouflage your approach the following morning.

13

Setting Up On Gobblers

The most important consideration when deciding where to set up to call in a gobbler is to know where a turkey *doesn't* want to walk. A gobbler prefers not to ...

... get his feet wet by crossing water.

... fly across water.

... walk through heavy cover or downhill.

... walk under a fence or fly over it.

... move into an area where he's encountered danger before.

... go into a region where he thinks another gobbler will beat him in a fight.

If a sportsman sets up in any of these areas and tries to call up a gobbler, chances are good that the bird won't come to him.

However, there are places a turkey enjoys walking. He is very apt to walk in a clean woods with little underbrush and in fields where he can see for great distances. He'll also walk on flat ground whenever possible.

And a turkey follows a regular routine. He's like the old man down the street who goes by the barber shop at 8:15 a.m., stops at the hardware store to find out if anyone's sick, dead or just married, swings by the coffee shop to pick up a newspaper and a sweet roll and then moves on to the fire station for a game of dominoes. You can set your watch by that old man.

You can also set your watch by an old gobbler in the spring.

That bird has a set routine as predictable as the man down the street. Figure out that pattern and you'll probably bag the bird. He will roost in the same tree, fly down in the same direction, try to mate in his strutting zones and feed in the same fields.

Once you know the routine, then it's time to plan the setup.

The Typical Set Up

One of the problems that a novice hunter has when setting up on gobblers is that he tries to get too close to the turkey. The result is that the bird spots the hunter and moves out of the area well before the hunter even tries to call him in.

Most often, this happens when a turkey gobbles in the direction of a hunter, turns around on the limb, faces the opposite direction and then gobbles away from the hunter. The bird then sounds farther away than he actually is. A good rule of thumb is to always set up farther away from the bird than you think you should.

Changing Locations

Although a turkey is sometimes taken on the first set up, it's by no means typical. More often than not, the hunter must set up two or three times to call the turkey.

Successfully changing calling locations is tricky, but the most important concern is knowing when to move and when to sit still. Many hunters spook a turkey when, after a few minutes of calling, the bird doesn't come in so the hunter gets up and moves to another location. Often, the hesitant gobbler is spooked by the impatient hunter.

There are times, however, when the hunter must move or else he won't get a gobbler. Maybe there's a creek or ditch that he doesn't know about. Perhaps the gobbler has encountered some hens and started to walk out of the area. The turkey may be call-shy because of other hunter encounters. Or the old bird may just be ornery and decide, "If that hen wants to be bred, she'll have to come find me."

When you move from spot to spot, change calls. Hopefully, the gobbler will think that there is yet another hen who is out looking for him. Sometimes, an aggressive hunter will change his position several times. But by moving, he often spooks the tom. Experienced hunters say that patience bags more gobblers than running and gunning.

A tree that is wider than your shoulders, open woods for the tom to walk through and a clear shooting lane are the essential elements to setting up for gobblers.

Setting Up On A Gobbler With Hens

One of the hardest gobblers to set up on and call to is the gobbler with hens. This gobbler already has what he's looking for and is reluctant to leave his harem just to meet and mate with a new lady friend. So the first few times you call, he probably won't come. But if you continue to call, his curiosity will get the best of him. There are three tactics that the hunter can use to take this gobbler.

1) Follow the gobbler through the woods as he moves with his hens. Stay out of sight, but continue to call to the gobbler using loud, demanding calls. Often, a gobbler will leave his hens or encourage his hens to walk with him to find the hunter he assumes to be another hen.

2) Most often, there will be a boss hen with the gobbler and several other hens. When you start giving a demanding call, the boss hen may answer your call as if to say, "This is my gobbler. You leave him alone." That's the time to forget about trying to talk to the gobbler and instead talk directly to the boss hen. Attempt to intimidate the boss hen and cause her to become so angry that she will come over to investigate the hen that's doing all the aggressive calling to her gobbler.

When she comes hunting the caller, she'll usually bring the harem of hens with her, and the tom should accompany her. Let the boss hen walk past without seeing you. The other hens will come into the area and so will the gobbler. When you get ready to make the shot, remember that more than one set of eyes are watching for movement. Numerous gobblers have been killed by hunters who called to the boss hen and then waited for the gobbler to follow.

3) If the boss hen is ready to be bred, she may answer your aggressive calling but not leave the gobbler to investigate. Then you must talk with both the hen and the gobbler. When the hen calls, call back aggressively. The instant the tom quits gobbling, start calling to him. If you want to talk to both, each time one of them calls, call back. This should excite either the hen or the gobbler. If the boss hen won't leave the gobbler, the longbeard will usually herd the boss hen over to the hunter.

Setting Up On A Gobbler That's Across The Water

One of the hardest turkey to set up on is the turkey that's across a body of water. Turkey, generally, don't like to fly across water to meet a hen, and most of the time they won't. But if there's a turkey

If the hunter sets up in an area where the tom is accustomed to walking, the bird will not be as wary about coming in close.

gobbling on the other side of a creek that you can't swim or refuse to wade, there are two techniques you can try.

1) Start calling aggressively with cuts, cackles and excited yelping. Put some emotion in those calls. You want to make the gobbler think there's a hen that's so excited about breeding that she just can't stand it. Frequently, a gobbler will become just as excited and drum and strut in hopes of getting the hen to fly across the creek to him.

Once you've got the turkey fired up and know he can't see you, start calling and moving away from the edge of the riverbank. This will create a picture in the gobbler's mind of a hen that's ready and wanting to breed. But since the tom won't fly across the creek to meet her, she's going to walk off and locate a gobbler on her side of the water. Hopefully, the gobbler won't be able to stand the pressure of that hen walking away, and will fly across the creek.

Be sure to listen for the gobbler's beating wings, because sometimes a longbeard will fly right to the caller.

2) If a turkey is hung up across water you must paint a picture in that gobbler's mind of a harem of hens that are excited and ready to breed. Imitate a one man band, cutting and cackling with a diaphragm call, while yelping and cutting on a box call. Then change calls and try to sound like a whole flock of hens, each with a different voice and excited about mating. Often, a gobbler that hears that much hen talk on the other side of a creek just can't stand the pressure. He believes that some gobbler will breed those hens in a short time and that it might just as well be himself, even if he has to fly across the creek for the date.

Setting Up On Gobblers Strutting In The Field

The gobbler strutting in the field is often the easiest turkey to find but can be the most difficult bird to set up on and call. Usually when a tom is out in the field, he either has hens with him or is in a place where hens should come. The natural order of things is that when a hen sees a gobbler, she should go to him. There are three ways to set up and take this type of tom.

1) A Daylight Field Gobbler is a tom that flies from the roost at daylight, remains in a field all day long and then flies back to the roost at dark. He's a difficult bird to kill. However, if the hunter reaches the field before daylight and takes a stand 10-15 yards in the woods off the edge of the field, he can confuse a gobbler and make him come to his call. Once the hunter has taken a stand, he can begin to call to the gobbler before daylight, before the tom has started gobbling or any other hens have awakened. The hunter should begin his calling just as light is beginning to glow in the east. When the bird wakes up and hears a hen calling to him from the field before fly-down time, he wonders if there's a new hen moving into his area. He'll often fly down from the roost to meet her before the other hens wake up.

2) In the middle of the day, especially late in the season, hens will leave a gobbler by 10:00 a.m. to return to their nests, which leaves the gobbler all alone in the field. If the hunter takes a stand 30-40 yards off the field and begins calling and using light yelps, clucks and purrs, he can get the gobbler's attention and make the tom believe that there's one hen left to breed before the day is over.

3) If there are three or four gobblers in a field with a group of hens, the hunter may have a chance to take a subordinate bird. Remember that since the boss gobbler claims the right to breed the

hens, subordinate toms may not have had an opportunity to breed any of the hens in the field. Therefore, if you set up fairly close to one of these subordinate gobblers that's not strutting, you may be able to call him to your blind.

Setting Up On Walking And Talking Gobblers

There's nothing more frustrating than to find a good gobbling bird, call to him and then listen to him walk off. In many instances these turkey are call-shy because they've listened to so much calling from other hunters that they know what a turkey call sounds like and don't want any part of it. Or maybe walking and talking gobblers just don't like hens. They'll gobble good but won't come to calling. There are two methods you can use to bag one of these walking and talking gobblers.

1) Circle the gobbler and take a stand in the woods where you think the turkey is going. Don't call to the turkey any more and the tom should come in silently. For some people, this is a boring way to hunt, but this technique can be successful.

2) Use two hunters. The first hunter takes a stand close to where the turkey is gobbling and then calls to the tom, just enough to keep the bird gobbling. The other hunter circles the turkey, gets in front of the tom and keeps up with his location as the turkey answers the caller. This too, will pay gobbler dividends.

Setting Up On The Hung-Up Gobbler

What should you do if a longbeard is standing 70 yards in front of you strutting, drumming and doing everything a wild turkey gobbler is supposed to do? First off, it's important to understand why a turkey hangs up out of shotgun range. Perhaps the hunter has called too much and the gobbler thinks that, "If that hen is so excited about mating, she ought to come to me when she hears me drum. I'm not going any closer to her."

Another possibility is that you're calling from a location where the tom has been shot at or attacked by a predator. Or perhaps the turkey spotted something, like movement when you sat down, the glint off the gun's barrel or a camo pattern that doesn't match the woods. A gobbler also knows that when he starts to strut he should be able to see the hen. For some reason, the tom has held up out of gun range. Here are two techniques you can try to get close enough for a shot.

1) Call to the bird with soft clucks and purrs with a different

call—try a slate call rather than the mouth diaphragm. The tom, however, might still refuse to move closer.

Probably the best tactic to use is to quit calling and allow the bird to settle down. Hopefully, he'll assume that the hen has left him, and walk away. Once the tom is well out of sight, circle the bird and try to set up a calling position parallel to the direction you think the turkey went. Change calls and begin calling very softly. Since the gobbler was already fired up, it's best to call very little.

2) Let's say that a bird hangs up just out of range. You quit calling and he walks off. Although you would like to follow him, you must get back for work. The following morning, set up closer to or actually in the area where the gobbler was strutting the day before. Since the tom thinks that the area is safe even with a hunter calling from that area, he may come in without any problem.

Setting Up Two Hunters On One Tom

One of the best reasons to hunt with a partner is that you can enjoy the natural camaraderie that results when two people pit their skills against one gobbler. For obvious safety reasons, be sure to keep visual contact with each other.

1) *With The Beginner.* Something magical happens to the beginner when he sees his first strutting bird. The result, at times, is that sanity and rationality take a vacation. For that reason, it's often best to place the experienced hunter in complete control. Many like to sit against a tree and have the novice sit between their legs. This way, it's easy for the two to communicate. The experienced hunter can simply whisper or tap the beginner to inform him of the distance to the bird and when to shoot.

2) *Shooter Out Front.* If you're hunting with a veteran hunter who's planning to shoot while you call, one option is to put him 15-20 yards in front of you. He already knows what to look for and when to shoot—you won't have to tell him the distance. Your job will be to concentrate on calling the bird. Because the tom expects the hen to be another 20 yards away, he will be less wary as he passes the veteran hunter in search of the hen. Also, if the tom hangs up 50 yards in front of you, your partner might still be close enough for a shot.

3) *Side By Side.* One technique favored by some experienced hunting partners is to hunt side by side. Both hunters sit with their backs to the same tree. They sit close enough so they can whisper back and forth as a turkey comes near. Whichever side the turkey comes in on, that hunter gets the shot.

14

How To Miss A Bird

I've missed two turkey in my life, and I remember both of them better than any turkey I've ever taken. The first bird was back in the late '60s after my college buddies had taught me to call. I was using a slate call, and had practiced for two months before winning the approval of my college cohorts. They, by contrast, were master turkey hunters. All of these guys were from rural Alabama where turkey hunting and turkey calling was as much a part of a boy's development as walking or running.

On the first afternoon of turkey season, I went into the Tombigbee River bottom swamps. I made several loud yelps, a few clucks, looked at my watch for ten minutes, and then repeated the sequence. After ten more minutes I hadn't heard a turkey gobble. So I got up and quietly walked down the road.

I'd gone about 30 yards when I noticed a large, dark shadow moving through an acorn flat not 30 yards from me. I squatted down and looked to see a longbeard gobbler headed straight to where I'd been calling. Although the bird was 30-35 yards away, I brought my gun to my shoulder and fired. The turkey took to the air, I fired two more times. The bird vanished just over a ridge on the other side of a waist-deep slough. Everything happened so fast that I wasn't sure whether I'd hit the turkey. I replayed the episode in my mind and then decided that I'd either killed or wounded the bird. That left only one option: wade the slough.

Just because springtime in the South feels warm doesn't mean that a sufficient amount of sunlight strikes the water to warm it. When I went into the cold slough to recover my turkey, I found out how frigid the water can be. I reached the other side of the slough, dripping wet but full of anticipation.

As I eased over a knoll, I spotted the gobbler. He took off on a dead run. I turned and slushed my way back to the car.

For the next 20 years I didn't fail to bag any bird that walked into my gun sights. Until the spring of 1988.

I had just scaled a mountain near Raton, New Mexico, and was breathing hard. My gun rested on my knee, my cheek was down and my eyes focused on a giant Merriam gobbler not more than 25 yards away. My hunting companion, Dale Faust, sat next to me.

"Shoot! John," he whispered.

But the turkey was behind a tree. He was also in full strut. I waited for him to break the strut and stick his neck straight up so that I'd have a better target. As I leaned out and around a tree, he broke his strut and put his neck straight up, alarmed at spotting my move. Faust hadn't brought his gun to his shoulder. He knew this was an easy shot, one I should have no trouble making.

I fired. But instead of falling over, the turkey ducked and ran.

Faust picked up his gun, fired and missed. We both jumped up to chase the gobbler. But before I could get my feet under me, I crashed headlong into a pine tree and saw those little white spots before my eyes that football players see when they get their bells rung. I staggered for a few minutes, then regained my feet. I took off on a dead run, chasing that tom and hoping that maybe Faust or I had inflicted a mortal wound. But as we watched, the tom ran off the side of the mountain, took to the air and flew away.

What happened next was the most humiliating moment in my whole career of turkey hunting. Faust looked back at me in disbelief and asked, "What happened?" I tried every excuse I could think of to explain the miss, but none of my excuses stood up to the close scrutiny of this master woodsman.

We returned to the tree I was leaning against when I shot, and I replayed the shot. As I leaned around the tree with my gun at my shoulder and attempted to aim, Faust said, "That's it, you're canting your shotgun."

I looked down and noticed I had rolled the gun off the side of my shoulder. When I was looking at the turkey, the shotgun was pointing about two feet to the other side of the bird.

No one should miss this shot. But it happens every day during the turkey season. With close shots like this your aim must be perfect because the pattern will open very little.

Let's look at some of the other ways that hunters miss or wound wild turkey.

Misjudging Distance

Knowing the distance to the turkey is critical for accurate shooting. If the tom is farther away than expected, your pattern will be too open for a killing shot. If by chance pellets do hit the head and neck area, they may lack the velocity to penetrate and cause enough damage to kill the bird. On the other hand, if you think the bird is 30 yards away, but he is actually 15 yards away, your pattern will open very little by the time it collides with the bird. Your shot, therefore, must be right on.

Shooting The Wrong Target

When the novice sees his first bird strutting at 30 yards sanity may take flight. The result is a belief that, "As big as that bird is and as close as he is, there's no way I can miss. I'll just point and squeeze the trigger. The turkey will fall over dead." This reasoning is the same kind of logic that makes novice quail hunters point amongst a covey of quail as they burst into the air. But as experienced bird hunters know, rarely does a covey shooter bag a bird unless he aims at a specific one.

Even though a wild turkey is a large target, to kill the gobbler you must shoot at a very small target: the turkey's head. If you shoot directly at the head, one half of the shot pattern will pass over it. Instead, shoot at the waddles on the turkey's neck where the skin joins the feathers. Then, depending on the pattern and distance, the entire shot pattern should cover the top of the turkey's head to the base of the turkey's neck. If you can get one pellet in the brain or in the spinal column, the bird should go down.

Not Seeing The Aiming Point

When a wild turkey comes in to a caller, the hunter recognizes that not only can the bird see better than he can, but that bird is also searching for movement, specifically a hen that he can't find. Therefore, any mistake that the hunter makes will spook the bird.

As a gobbler comes in, the hunter should concentrate on ...

... where he should allow the bird to get to before he tries to bag him.

... whether there are bushes or trees between him and the gobbler that will hinder his shot.

... when he can move into a shooting position.

Before you shoot at a trotting bird, make sure that no brush or branches are in the way of your shot. The head and neck of a turkey are small and every pellet from your shot is important.

... whether the turkey will break his strut.

... how far the shot is, and whether he should take it.

While all this is going through the turkey hunter's mind, he must also remember to push off the safety, get his cheek on the stock, look straight down the barrel, superimpose the bead on the turkey's neck and squeeze the trigger. With all this information being processed, it's easy to understand how one or two steps can be left out.

For instance, perhaps the hunter doesn't have his cheek down. Instead, his head might be up, looking at the bird. The result will be a miss. Or perhaps the hunter aims correctly, but doesn't see a small twig, a little tree or a limb between the bead and the tom. Often the brain is concentrating so hard on the bead of the shotgun and the turkey's neck that it doesn't process the information provided by the eyes.

Although there are many reasons that a hunter can miss, even if he does hit the gobbler, he may only wound the bird instead of bringing him down. Turkey are tough birds. Unless a hunter puts a hard lick on the gobbler, the turkey will recover. If the hunter shoots the turkey anywhere except the head and neck, there's a good chance that the bird's feathers and wings will absorb the shot and prevent it from puncturing the turkey's body. Or if the shot does pierce the turkey's body, the pellets won't penetrate far enough to harm a vital organ.

Arrowing A Gobbler

Sometimes, bowhunters have been criticized for attempting to bag turkey with a bow. A bow doesn't have the knockdown power of a shotgun. Also, the bowhunter is shooting to penetrate the turkey's body cavity and cause enough damage to the internal organs to stop the bird. However, these organs are small, and a turkey doesn't bleed like a deer or other big game animal. The result, sometimes, is a lost bird.

Therefore, if you're going to hunt turkey with a bow a string tracker is an absolute must. Also, the arrow should have a device to keep the broadhead in the gobbler and inflict more damage. It's also best to wait for at least 20 minutes after you've arrowed a gobbler. Allow the turkey to succumb to the deadly effects of the arrow before you pursue it. Your chances of recovering the tom will be much greater.

15

Turkey Decoys

Turkey decoys are a recent addition to the sport of turkey hunting. The decoy gives the gobbler something to see, which up until this point had only been a promise that the hunter created by calling. But now the decoy attracts the gobbler and keeps his attention away from the hunter.

There are several types of turkey decoys and tactics that can be used. In some states decoying is permitted, while it is banned in others. *Be sure to check your local regulations.* The use of live decoys is banned in every state. But in some states that permit decoys the hunter can use a mounted bird. If a state allows the hunter to harvest a hen turkey, he has access to one of the most successful decoys: a mounted hen turkey. One of the best hen mounts is with her standing, neck down, as though she's about to feed. A taxidermist can put wires through the hen's feet and legs. The hunter can stick these wires in the ground for a standing decoy. Another option is to leave the feet of the mounted bird an inch or two off the ground. Then tie a black string to the hen's foot. By pulling lightly on the string, the turkey will rock back and forth and appear to be pecking. This decoy may lure in even the most cantankerous gobbler.

However, having a hen turkey mounted by a reputable taxidermist can be expensive. One possibility is to find someone who is interested in taxidermy but has never mounted a turkey.

You can pay for the supplies, while the novice learns his craft. The apprentice taxidermist experiences mounting a hen at no cost, and you get a decoy that may not look perfect but is lifelike.

Even though a mounted hen is the best decoy, a mounted gobbler can work just as well and probably will be much easier to obtain than a mounted hen.

To acquire a mounted gobbler check at yard sales and ask around at local sporting goods shops. When you locate a "used" mounted gobbler its condition will explain why it has little value. Although many of these old mounts are hideous-looking, they still make excellent decoys. If you decide to buy a mounted turkey at a yard sale, *check the laws in your state to be certain that the buying and selling of mounted turkey is legal.* If the condition of the mount is too poor to use as a decoy, break the wings off and use them to beat the ground when you give the fly-down cackle. Your fly-down cackle and the wings beating against the ground should increase the gobbler's excitement and bring him to the gun.

In recent years, many companies have made plastic decoys that resemble hen turkey. These decoys can be stuck into the ground where the gobbler can see them. They are effective, lightweight and easier to carry than mounted birds. Plus, they aren't damaged as easily in rain and foul weather. Many hunters believe that plastic decoys are just as effective as mounted birds.

How To Safely Use Decoys

When a hunter moves through the woods, he sounds like a turkey. And when he gives turkey calls, it's easy for other hunters to think that he is a turkey. With his camo clothing and low position to the ground, he can even look like a turkey. But when the hunter goes one step further and puts a turkey decoy in front of him, he has all the ingredients to be mistaken for a big gobbler. It's tough for any hunter to recommend using a turkey decoy on public land, because it's impossible to know if there are other hunters in the woods. Even on private land, turkey decoys can be deadly. I'm very reluctant to use them and very cautious if I do. To be safe, carry the decoy in some type of orange wrapper when moving in and out of the woods.

Where To Place the Decoy

For a turkey decoy to be effective, it must be placed where the gobbler can see it and naturally expects another turkey. Therefore, don't situate the decoy in thick cover or close to a bush. One of the

A decoy will attract and keep a tom's interest. Notice the hunter at the edge of the trees who is able to draw a bead on this gobbler without being noticed.

problems that most hunters encounter who have never used a decoy is that they put their decoy too close to the blind. The idea is that if the gobbler comes in, the decoy will bring him even closer. However, even if the gobbler sees another turkey, he may be reluctant to come in to what he assumes to be a danger area. So locate your decoy in plain sight at least 10 to 20 yards away from your blind.

Be sure to position the decoy with its head turned in the opposite direction from which you expect the tom. Then when the gobbler comes in and attempts to make eye contact with the decoy, he won't be alerted by those cold, dead eyes. Also, since the decoy is facing away from the tom, he may assume that the decoy is either disinterested or doesn't see him, which may cause him to come in quicker and be less wary.

Sometimes gobblers do strange things to decoys. I've heard reports of gobblers mounting decoys, tearing them up and fighting with them. So if you have a nice mount, you may want to harvest the gobbler before he dukes it out with your decoy.

It's also safe to say that the less time a turkey has to study the decoy, the more likely he is to be fooled by it. Set the decoy up so that just as the turkey comes over a rise 40 or 50 yards away he will see the decoy. Usually, he will walk right in.

Bowhunting With A Decoy

One of the fairest uses of a decoy is when bowhunting, because a bowhunter has the odds stacked against him. Usually he must stand up to take a gobbler, which means the turkey is more likely to see him than if he's sitting on the ground with a firearm. Also, a bowhunter makes several moves when he draws, aims and shoots. And the bowhunter must have the turkey within 30 yards. With these factors against the bowhunter, a turkey decoy offers some relief.

How To Decoy The Tough Tom

In areas with a lot of hunting pressure, longbeards are quick to wise up. They've been educated by hunters, know the difference between a hunter and a hen, and often refuse to answer a call. To bag a tough tom, set out a decoy and call lightly. Sometimes the tom will silently come in, never making a sound but cautiously looking for a hen.

16

Fall Hunting

Why do some states have fall turkey seasons while others do not? At first glance it would seem that those states with a large turkey population use fall turkey seasons as a management tool to control the flocks. Those states without a fall season must not have a large enough population to support the season. Although this seems like the obvious answer, it's usually not that simple.

Take, for example, Alabama. Alabama has one of the largest turkey flocks in the nation. And yet only 12 of its 67 counties have a fall turkey season. To rephrase the first question of this chapter: Why do some counties have fall turkey seasons while other counties in the same state do not?

The Tradition

Even before a child goes to school, he learns that on the first Thanksgiving Day the founding fathers had a celebration with the Indians to give thanks for their safe arrival to the new world and their newfound freedom. The main course on the menu for that first Thanksgiving dinner was wild turkey. Today, many folks have dubbed Thanksgiving Day as "Turkey Day."

Nobody needs a Ph.D. in American history to figure out that if the Pilgrims and Indians celebrated Thanksgiving in November those turkey were killed in the fall. So the logical sequence is that the traditional time to hunt turkey is in the fall.

One of the strongest motivations for doing anything is tradition. The 12 Alabama counties that have fall turkey seasons, in most cases, have always had a fall season. It's the tradition, and with a strong turkey population, there is little reason to break that tradition.

An additional reason for the continued fall season is that during the fall the turkey are not breeding. The result is that the season is less likely to impact on the turkey that are produced during the breeding season. Also, some sportsmen enjoy hunting other species at the same time as they hunt turkey.

Another position is that more skill is required to find and bag a gobbler in the fall than in the spring. Toms are not gobbling in the fall. So the hunter must locate the turkey, scatter the flock and then call the birds back together. Rather than calling the gobbler to him with seductive hen calls, he must discover where the tom wants to go and then set up an ambush along the route that the turkey will take.

These are logical, rational reasons that sportsmen use in various states to secure a fall turkey season.

Reasons Against A Fall Season

The case against a fall turkey season is usually voiced by purist turkey hunters. In many areas of the country, turkey hunting is like a sacred ritual, a practice that must abide by the strictest rules. Sometimes, the personal rules of the purist are imposed on the other turkey hunters in that area.

One question they ask is: At what age should a gobbler be sent to his happy roosting tree in the sky? It is answered in several ways. One group responds by saying, "Anytime I can legally harvest a gobbler, I should be able to take the bird." That's not a bad attitude since game is a renewable resource.

Another group says that, "I don't want to shoot a one year old (jake) gobbler, because they're juvenile birds and not challenging to hunt. I'd rather let that bird live another year and be a two year old before I take him. I enjoy hunting the smarter, two year old birds."

This hunter has set a standard for himself, which is fine. A large percentage of turkey hunters follow this rule. But having this attitude does not mean that this sportsman deserves a higher place in the pecking order of turkey hunters than the person who harvests a jake.

The third type of sportsman, who has a more restrictive view of

Nobody needs a Ph.D. in American history to figure out that if the Pilgrims and Indians celebrated Thanksgiving in November those turkey were killed in the fall. The traditional time to hunt turkey is during the fall.

when a gobbler should be harvested, believes that, "I don't want to take a gobbler unless he has at least one-inch spurs. I've killed enough toms to know I'm a turkey hunter, and I only want to hunt trophy birds that are three years old or older. Therefore I'll pass up all the jakes and two year old birds that others hunt and only pit my skills against the biggest, oldest and most challenging gobblers."

The fourth kind of turkey hunter is much like the gunslinger of the Old West and prefers only to hunt and bag the legends—the gobblers that have outsmarted every turkey hunter in the area. These legendary birds are challenging for the experienced gobbler chaser. His position is that, "I want to take the turkey that nobody can harvest and pit my skills against the very best turkey in the country. And when I take one of those tough birds, I'll know I've reached the highest level of turkey hunting."

Now that we understand the different attitudes of turkey hunters concerning when a gobbler should be bagged, let's look at fall turkey hunting.

In the fall, the primary social need of all turkey is to flock together, and both males and females will remain in large flocks. To harvest a turkey in the fall, most hunters first scatter the flock and then give the assembly call of the old hen or the kee-kee run. The first turkey to respond to the assembly call are the young gobblers and hens. It's a call from the hen to gather her young. The kee-kee run is the young gobbler's squealing call that's given by the jakes to keep up with each other, the flock and their mothers.

When the hunter gives either of these two calls, he's primarily talking to the juvenile birds. The turkey that most often come to this type of calling are the jakes. Although older, longbeard gobblers are taken in the fall, they are usually flushed by accident or taken while the hunter is hunting another species of game.

How To Bag A Longbeard In The Fall

Calling a longbeard in the fall is a difficult proposition. Here's why:

... The older gobbler doesn't have sex on his mind in the fall like he does in the spring. That means he'd rather hang around with the guys than associate with the hens.

... Turkey don't talk much in the fall. Therefore, calling a tom in is difficult.

... A lone gobbler in the fall more than likely wants to be by himself and won't respond to calling.

Although it is difficult, a small number of turkey hunters can

To harvest a turkey in the fall, most hunters scatter the flock and then give the assembly call of the old hen or the kee-kee run.

call in and bag a gobbler in the fall. Sometimes, a hunter can give coarse gobbler yelps to an older bird. If that older tom is in the mood for company, he may cautiously come to those yelps. But as a general rule, calling to the gobbler during the fall is one of the least effective methods of taking a mature gobbler.

The most efficient way to bag a longbeard in the fall is to decide where that turkey wants to go and take a stand along that route. If you're hunting in snow country, look for the turkey's trail in the snow and learn the routes he's taking. However, the hunter must remember that just because the season has changed, the turkey hasn't lost his wariness. Camouflage is still as critical to success as it was in the spring, except that now the hunter may want to use camo with white in it to match the background in which he must conceal himself.

In areas with large dairy farms, look for turkey sign near pastures. Turkey will feed on the undigested seeds in manure. Because the manure is not frozen—thus easy for the turkey to get at—it may be a popular feeding spot.

Another productive technique for hunting turkey in the fall is to talk to the wildlife biologist in the region you plan to hunt. He or she should be able to provide you with the types of feed the turkey prefer during the fall season. The biologist might also have information on which areas offer the preferred feed. Your local department of conservation is a valuable source of information.

17

The Guided Hunt

When it comes to turkey hunting, first-hand experience is the best teacher. The basic techniques and tactics can be understood by reading books and magazines. But turkey hunting knowledge is harder to come by. At which moment should you return a gobbler's call? Can you tell from the tom's gobble if he will move in closer? Is now a good time to switch calls, or is it time to sit tight and keep quiet? These are judgment calls. They are best learned under the canopy of the big sky.

It is possible to find answers to these questions without the help of anyone else. That will take time. Hunting with a guide will shorten the number of fruitless mornings the beginner spends in the woods. Even the experienced turkey hunter is occasionally humbled by a stubborn or call-shy gobbler. A guide can shed new insight on the sport or a seldom-used technique.

Where To Find A Turkey Guide

The first place to start your search for a good turkey hunting guide is the NAHC Approved Outfitters & Guides booklet. This book lists the guides that your fellow NAHC members have hunted with and recommend.

Turkey calling contests are not only one of the best places to learn how to call turkey, they're also a great place to find the area's most experienced guides. Most of the competitors at these contests also work as guides. So talk with the judges at these contests. Ask them to name the top three guides in the area. Then interview the people they recommend.

There are many good reasons to hire a guide. To list but a few, guides know the area you will be hunting and can take you to where the toms are located. The majority are excellent callers and will bring a tom within gun range. They can keep you from getting lost and show you which calls are most effective. In short, a guide will help you bag a gobbler and will provide you with valuable information about hunting turkey successfully.

An important question to ask a guide is whether he will carry a gun on your hunt. If he will, ask why. Some guides are concerned with their success rate. If a beginner cannot bag a tom, some guides may want to shoot a tom for the hunter. If that's agreed to by the hunter, then that's fine. But the hunter pays good money to hunt with a guide. The hunter should have the total experience of harvesting a gobbler, win, lose or draw. The guide's reputation of bagging a bird on every outing is not nearly as important as the experience the hunter gains.

How To Get The Most From Your Guided Hunt

The attitude that the hunter has toward a guide directly relates to the hunter's success and his comfort on the hunt. Remember that although a guide is a master of his sport, he may not be highly schooled, he may not use the language associated with genteel society and he may not dress like a corporate executive. However, in the woods the guide has as much knowledge, skill, and wisdom about turkey hunting as a corporate executive has about his corporation. The hunter who understands this and treats a guide with respect will be in the presence of a man who will walk across burning coals to produce a bird.

The little things are what make a guide's work tough. When a hunter puts his utmost confidence and trust in his guide and communicates that to the guide, then the guide will give all he has to locate a gobbler and aid the hunter in harvesting that turkey. And most guides will give more than is expected by spending extra time with the hunter teaching him how to hunt and explaining why the hunt was conducted the way it was.

Also, if the hunter has treated the guide with respect, most guides will carry the turkey out of the woods for the hunter, field dress the bird and ensure that the sportsman maximizes the enjoyment and pleasure of his hunt. If the hunter treats the guide as

Put your utmost confidence and trust in the guide and communicate that to him. In return, he will do all he can to help you bag a gobbler and teach you about the sport.

a friend rather than as a hired hand, he will be repaid in kind.

Hunting With Lodge Guides

One of the quickest ways to learn how to turkey hunt is stay at a commercial hunting lodge and pay the price for lodging, a guide and food. Most of these lodges have to maintain fine turkey flocks and expert guides to stay in business. The cost may be high, but after a week of hunting with a guide steeped in turkey hunting tactics who hunts gobblers every day of the season, you will be well on your way to mastering the sport yourself.

It's important to realize that most guides believe themselves to be master turkey hunters, excellent callers and superb woodsmen. The title ''guide'' reinforces a master woodsman's opinion of himself and is part of the basis of his turkey hunting reputation.

In any lodge, there's a pecking order among the guides. Most always one guide will consistently lead his customers to more turkey and is responsible for more birds being bagged than the rest of the guides. To be the number one guide, he must always work as hard as he can to help his clients bag their birds.

Meanwhile, the other guides in the lodge constantly are attempting to take over his position as number one. Therefore, they will do everything in their power to aid their clients in taking gobblers. Each time a guide comes in from a hunt with a successful hunter, he is king for a day at the lodge. And just like the majestic bird that's been bagged, the successful guide claims the right to strut his feathers and crow to the world of his prowess, superiority and mastery of the sport.

At the same time, the other unsuccessful guides resemble whipped dogs who've failed in their chosen vocation and are disappointed in their outdoor abilities. However, these unfortunate guides renew their confidence with statements like, "Well, we didn't get that bird this morning. But I've got him figured out now, and I feel sure we can bag that turkey in the morning." Or, "That bird gave us the slip. Although he's not acting like he should, I know where there's a bird we can take tomorrow," which is not mere guide talk. For a guide to continue his employment with any hunting lodge, he must produce birds for his clients. That's the bottom line. So if he's not productive for the lodge's customers, he very well may not be guiding the next season.

Therefore, there's good healthy competition between guides at a hunting lodge to help their hunters bag gobblers.

Buddy Hunting

Buddy hunting with a guide is an altogether different experience than paying someone to take you and teach you turkey hunting. If a hunter is willing to take another hunter, free of charge, on a turkey hunt with the understanding that, "Whichever one of us gets a shot, we'll take it," the novice hunter has an excellent opportunity to learn about turkey hunting.

In these situations, the novice frequently picks up all expenses. It's worth it! Any cost the beginner will incur is pittance compared to the knowledge gained.

18

Hunting In
The Face Of Danger

B ill was excited about hunting the turkey season opener with his son David. Both were good hunters. Both were productive callers. And both were planning to hunt the same river bottom swamp. They had scouted the area together and located several gobblers.

On opening morning Bill let David out of the truck, drove about two miles down the road, parked the truck and went into the woods. They each located a gobbler at daylight. But neither could bring the gobbler into gun range.

Then about 9:00 a.m., Bill heard a bird gobble and moved in to work the tom. As Bill was slipping into the area, he froze dead in his tracks. A gobbler was less than 30 yards away.

He waited until the turkey's back was to him. Then he brought the gun to his shoulder, took careful aim at the neck and squeezed the trigger.

The gun exploded. Then there was a scream, and Bill realized he had shot his son.

Today David is blind in one eye. This father and son have never reentered the woods to hunt wild turkey. Not only was the sport of turkey hunting lost for this outdoor family, but a young man lives his life in partial darkness. His father copes with the understanding that David was blinded by his mistake.

This accident was a terrible tragedy. The names for obvious

reasons have been changed. I tell this true story not to stop anyone from hunting turkey nor to terrorize fellow sportsmen. Rather, this story is told to emphasize the fact that turkey hunting can be a dangerous sport. Bill was not a novice turkey hunter. He had hunted springtime gobblers for more than 30 years. He knew what a turkey sounded like and looked like.

It seems that a sportsman with that much woods experience would not mistake another hunter for a bird. But according to the National Wild Turkey Federation, (NWTF) most turkey hunting accidents are caused by experienced hunters.

"A turkey hunt is like a jigsaw puzzle that has all the pieces laid before the sportsman," says Rob Keck, Executive Vice President of NWTF. "The more times the hunter has worked the puzzle, and the more of the puzzle parts he sees and understands, the quicker he is able to put the puzzle together. A hunter with less experience requires more time to piece the puzzle parts together and figure out the picture. However, when someone who has hunted turkey for years hears something that sounds like a turkey, sees an image that moves like a turkey and spots the colors that look like a turkey's head, the hunter completes the picture of a turkey. Sometimes he raises his gun and fires.

"The reason this happens is because a man walking through the woods sounds exactly like a wild turkey. If a man gobbles like a turkey, walks like a turkey, is camouflaged to fit in with his environment and is squatting or leaning against a tree, he can be mistaken for a wild turkey. Or perhaps he has a white t-shirt under his camouflage, a blue undershirt and/or a red or white handkerchief in his pocket. Then he shows the colors of a wild turkey, and the possibility exists for another hunter to put the puzzle parts together and mistake him for a turkey.

"*Turkey hunters must be the most cautious hunters in the woods.* They must expect, look for and assume that what they're seeing is actually another hunter rather than a turkey—until they're proven wrong."

No matter how safety-conscious a hunter thinks he is, he may someday be involved in an accident.

Here's another example: I love to hunt with my son, John. He carries my name, John Edward Phillips, Jr., and carries my spirit and love of the wild. Although John is only 14, he's already taken his first gobbler and has been hunting toms for three seasons. John knows the rules of safety. However this past spring, I was terrified at what I saw when we were hunting.

A turkey hunter calls like a turkey, sits in locations where other hunters expect to see a turkey and is camouflaged beyond recognition. No matter how safety-conscious a hunter thinks he is, he may someday be involved in an accident.

The morning was cool when we left camp on opening morning of Alabama's turkey season to hunt a gobbler we had spotted the day before. We both donned extra clothing because of the icy elements we would surely encounter.

At sunrise we heard a turkey gobble and set up next to a big beech tree. While I was putting on my gloves and headnet John adjusted his gear and donned his camouflage. I began to call, and we waited for the gobbler. As I called, we quietly discussed where we would take the shot and which way the bird might come in to us. Sitting shoulder to shoulder, we whispered without looking directly at one another.

As the first hour passed, the bird never showed up. But we had a good talk and enjoyed the quality time together. As with all fathers I love my son and feel that he's a part of my heart. We gathered our gear and got ready to leave. As I stood up and looked at John what I saw scared me beyond words.

Because the morning was cool, John had worn a blue, long-sleeved, hooded sweatshirt. When he donned his camouflage, John had pulled the hood of the sweatshirt up and had put his camo headnetting over it. Through the camo netting the blue hooded sweatshirt looked exactly like the blue on a turkey's head. If we had used a gobbling box to bring in that tom, we might have called in another hunter.

Be absolutely certain not to have any clothing or equipment that's either blue, white or red. Then there's no chance of showing the colors of a turkey's head. Buttons can come open or fall off; clothing can be torn to reveal what's underneath; or the wrong color of clothing can work its way to the surface. Eliminate any of the colors from your turkey hunting wardrobe that even slightly resemble a turkey's head.

Some people have suggested that turkey hunters should be required to wear hunter orange. Although the hunter will be safer wearing hunter orange, he rarely will see a turkey. Although turkey may appear to be less than intelligent at times, they're not stupid. Wearing hunter orange would not lend itself to many successful hunts. There is also the discussion in some hunting circles that hunter orange could eventually contribute to more accidents. The belief is that to a somewhat color blind hunter or in the early morning, orange might look like red. Since red is the color of a turkey's head, they say, even more hunters could be mistaken for wild turkey.

The hunter is most often mistaken for a gobbler when he gives

Every hunter should be absolutely certain that neither his clothing nor his equipment has any blue, white or red. Then there's no chance of showing the colors of a turkey's head.

a gobbling call. This is the most dangerous call because the sportsman is imitating the bird that other hunters in the woods are trying to bag. *Only give a gobbling call when your back is against a tree that's larger than your shoulders, and you're in a region where you can see extremely well in all directions.*

Here's a scenario to better protect yourself: Tim is sitting next to a tree larger than his shoulders in a place where he can see in all directions. Since he has a gobbling turkey in front of him that won't come in, he gives the gobble call to draw the longbeard into gun range. Just after he makes the gobbling call, he sees another hunter slip into his area and set up beside a tree not 30 yards away.

This second hunter—let's call him Ed—doesn't see Tim. Both can hear the turkey drum and strut as the bird moves closer. Tim is faced with a difficult decision. Does he wait for the gobbler to move to within gun range, which probably will be only a matter of seconds? Or does he signal Ed and let him know his location? In doing so he may spook the bird.

Many thoughts go through Tim's mind. He has been trying to get a shot at this bird for a week. He's been hunting that bird all morning and realizes that in a few seconds he could take the bird. Although he thinks that Ed shouldn't have come into his area, he also believes that if he'll just wait, the turkey will show up and he can shoot the bird. That will signal Ed. Tim is convinced that there is no way Ed can mistake him for a tom. Surely he can hear the gobbler dragging his wings through the leaves as he struts.

Tim is playing a dangerous, stupid game. Any time a sportsman lets a turkey rob him of safe hunter practices, he is mentally and emotionally incompetent and has taken leave of his senses. No turkey is worth getting shot. Any time a hunter enters another hunter's area, both must know each other's location. Otherwise, it's an accident waiting to happen. Your family will be more proud if you arrive home alive than if you take a turkey and put yourself in the eye of danger. *Don't let a gobbler rob you of your sanity.* Always put safety first and turkey taking second.

The Old Man And The Bird

"We can't go hunting this afternoon," a friend told me one afternoon during turkey season. "Old Mr. Smith who owns the hardware store went out turkey hunting this morning and didn't come back. He's got a heart condition and his family is afraid that he had a heart attack in the woods. The sheriff is organizing a search party and he's asked all the boys here at the college to help.

Get your compass and your flashlight, and put on your boots and a blaze orange shirt. We've got to find Mr. Smith.''

The search began at about 2:00 p.m. It was one of those jobs you do, not because you want to, but because someday you may need similar help. I dreaded the thought of finding Mr. Smith dead next to a tree. He was a fine friend who had willingly shared his turkey hunting experience.

We began the search, and kept at it all afternoon. As the search wore on and darkness fell, hope of Mr. Smith's survival dwindled. However, when we checked back in at 11:00 p.m., Mr. Smith had been found. He was hungry and worn out, but in good shape for the ordeal he had endured.

In pursuit of a gobbler, Mr. Smith had become lost in what to him were familiar woods. When he couldn't find his way out of the woods that afternoon, he had sat down next to a tree. Tired and exhausted, he had fallen asleep. When he woke up, the woods were dark. Mr. Smith didn't know where to go or how to get back to his vehicle. So he did the right thing by staying where he was and waiting to be found.

No sportsman ever plans to get lost while turkey hunting. Most turkey hunters plan to go right to a gobbler that he located when scouting, sit down and call the bird to him. However, when this plan doesn't work, he may walk from five to 15 miles, either trying to find a turkey or moving from gobbling turkey to gobbling turkey.

Some woodsmen have a better sense of direction than others. They can go into the woods before daylight and come out after dark at the exact same spot. Others aren't that skilled. Even a master woodsman should ''plan'' on getting lost. He will take a compass reading to know which direction the road runs. He will have an aerial photo of the region. He'll also carry a flashlight, waterproof matches, emergency blanket, length of lightweight rope and several candy bars.

Presuming that he will get lost and carrying survival gear does not show a lack of confidence on the sportsman's part. Instead it shows level-headedness and experience.

Buddy Hunting Safety

Hunter safety is not only applicable for a sportsman looking out for himself, but he must also be responsible for his hunting companion. Even though the hunter may not be involved in an accident, he may have to care for a buddy who is injured, lost or incapacitated.

Therefore when a hunter takes survival gear with him into the woods, he's doing it not only for himself but also for the ones with whom he's hunting. If a friend falls and breaks his leg, nightfall may catch the two hunting partners well away from medical aid. That's when building a campfire, having some candy bars to share and making a splint with sticks and a lightweight rope will add comfort to a bad situation. Even a few bandaids in a survival kit may reduce the pain of a minor cut, blister or skinned knee. Carrying a suvival pack is just common sense when turkey hunting.

19

After The Shot

When the hunter squeezes the trigger and the bird flops, the hunt is over. But then the decision must be made about what to do with the bird. Is the turkey to be mounted or eaten? If the tom is to be mounted, run to the gobbler as soon as the trigger is pulled, grab the turkey by the feet or the head, and hold the tom up off the ground. Then if the turkey is flopping, he won't knock a large portion of his feathers off.

Field care for a bird that is to be mounted begins immediately. The less damage the turkey does to his feathers, the better the mount. If any of the tail or wing feathers are shot off or broken, gather up these feathers as they may be able to be replaced by a competent taxidermist.

Also the decision to mount or eat the bird dictates whether or not the gobbler should be field dressed. To be mounted, a gobbler doesn't need to be field dressed. If the turkey is to be eaten, field dressing it is appropriate.

The decision will also determine how the bird is transported out of the woods. If the bird is to be mounted, all care should be taken to protect the feathers and to keep any blood from drying on them. If the turkey will be dinner, then the condition of the feathers is not important.

The Turkey For Mounting

A mounted wild turkey is one of the most beautiful trophies a hunter can collect. Persuading other people that this is true can be simple. The classic example is the sportsman who brought a 20-pound bird with a nine-inch beard and one-inch spurs into a taxidermy shop.

Although the hunter was excited about having the bird mounted, he had a problem. "My wife, who is an artist, has beautiful paintings hung all over our home," he said. "She doesn't want me to have this turkey mounted, and she told me I'd either have to hang it in the basement or in my office. I don't know what to do with the bird."

He was undecided at first, but then he decided to have the turkey mounted in a flying position.

Several months later when the gobbler was ready the taxidermist called his home. He was out of town, but his wife reluctantly agreed to pick up the tom. As she walked into the taxidermist's shop she stopped in the doorway and looked as though she had seen either an angel or a ghost. Then she asked, "Is that my husband's turkey?"

"Yes ma'am," he said, trying to understand whether she was happy or upset.

"Why, that's the most beautiful thing I've ever seen in my life. Look at how the feathers catch the light and how the different hues of copper, gold and green are reflected. I never knew turkey were so beautiful. Can I borrow your phone?"

As the taxidermist listened the wife, who was formerly reluctant to place a mounted turkey in her home, called an electrician and explained that he must come immediately to install three types of spotlights to highlight the wall where she planned to hang the turkey.

A couple of weeks later, her husband dropped into the taxidermy shop and said, "You won't believe what my wife did with that turkey. She took her favorite painting off the wall and hung my gobbler in its place! Then she called all the neighbors and invited them over to see, 'Our turkey.' I don't believe my wife could have been more pleased with a pair of diamond earrings than she was with that mounted turkey. She just couldn't believe that anything found in the woods could be that pretty."

Once a sportsman decides to mount a turkey, he has several options including whether to have the bird strutting, standing or flying. The place where a hunter intends to display the bird may

As soon as you squeeze the trigger and see the tom tumble, run to him. Many wounded birds have returned to their feet and led hunters on a long, frustrating chase.

Once you reach the downed bird, firmly step on his head.

dictate which mount he chooses. If the tom is to be set on the floor, the hunter must consider if he has small children, dogs or cats. Children and pets will run into, bump into and sometimes tear up mounted animals left standing on the floor.

However, if the sportsman has solved the problem of where to put his mount, then the space the bird will take up when it is strutting or standing is an additional consideration. Also, a turkey mounted flying will require an expanse of wall space, since the wingspan of many gobblers may be four or five feet.

Next, the hunter must decide how to have the turkey's head preserved. There are three different methods of mounting the turkey's head. Some taxidermists skin out the head, preserve the skin and then restretch the skin over some type of mannequin. This method has been used for many years. But often the turkey's head will crack.

Another technique uses either a rubber or plastic head in place of the real head and solves the cracking problem. But some heads look very artificial.

The third and best method is to freeze-dry the turkey's head. This takes longer, but ensures that the head won't crack and will appear lifelike.

Determining the color of the gobbler's head is the next hurdle the customer and the taxidermist face. To make the head look lifelike, the head must be painted. Each individual has his own opinion of the colors on a turkey's head. As biologists point out, a turkey's head can be many different colors. You've probably seen turkey with solid red, white or blue heads as well as all of those colors mixed and shaded. Therefore, look at turkey heads the taxidermist has already painted and mounted. Then you'll get a feel for what the head on your gobbler will look like once the job is completed.

Something else a turkey hunter must consider is the cost of the mount. Prices vary, but generally the higher the cost, the higher the quality.

Price should not be the sole factor that determines whether or not a bird is to be mounted. When a hunter weighs all the other costs involved in bagging a bird, the cost of having the turkey mounted may be one of the cheapest expenses. To decide the true value of a trophy bird, add up the amount of money you have invested in clothing, calls, hunting leases, hunting vehicles and decoys. Add to that the number of hours spent learning to call and hunting. The bottom line is that mounting the turkey is often the least expensive part of the hunt.

Once the trophy has been hung or placed in the sportsman's home, all that's required to keep the bird clean is an occasional dusting with a soft feather duster.

The Other Trophies

Mounting the entire turkey is not the turkey hunter's only option. The turkey has many interesting parts that can be used for decorative purposes. Often I'll include a turkey's colorful breast or back feather in a letter to a turkey hunting friend, another writer, a manufacturer of turkey hunting accessories or just someone I think will enjoy the beauty of the feather.

A turkey's feathers can be crafted into earrings and necklaces that make perfect Christmas gifts. By gluing the feathers to some colorful beads and the beads to an earring post, the sportsman can fashion an inexpensive present that says more than, "I went to the store and bought you this." And the turkey hunter can use clear lacquer to polish the gobbler's spurs, which then can be attached to earring posts or crafted into necklaces. Also, the turkey's toenails can be polished and made into dainty earrings.

A gobbler's feet can be dried and preserved, and by using wire and a lamp fixture will make lamps or hat racks. A tom's tail can be fanned and dried and made into a beautiful wall hanging. The

With your foot on the tom's head, grab the feet and lift up.

feathers along the turkey's back as they meet the neck also make nice wall hangings. Skin that platelet of feathers from the neck to the tail, and then preserve that skin with a dry preservative that can be purchased from your local taxidermy service to create another unusual wall hanging.

Or you can skin out turkey wings on the back side, remove the meat, and add the same dry preservative to the skin and bones of the wings. Then stretch out these wings to be either mounted on the wall or used to help call in turkey. After giving the fly-down cackle the hunter can beat the wings against the ground to imitate the sound of the wild turkey hen when she flies from the roost down to the ground. So just because a hunter decides not to get his b. mounted doesn't mean that he doesn't have any trophies to preserve and keep.

The Gobbler To Eat

Most people are convinced that the wild turkey is some of the best tablefare a sportsman can bring home from the woods. The care that bird is given in the field has an effect on the way the meat tastes when it's brought to the table. Most often, simply field dress the turkey by cutting a hole around the anus and reaching in and removing all the entrails.

One mistake that turkey hunters often make is to wash out the cavity with creek or stream water. Do not wash the inside of the bird until the tom is ready to be cooked or frozen. If the hunter puts water inside the turkey's cavity, bacteria can begin to grow rapidly. So by merely taking the entrails out, the hunter can lighten the load he must carry from the woods and prevent a souring on the inside of the bird.

Some hunters, especially if they've bagged a gobbler deep in the woods, will breast the turkey like a dove hunter breasts a dove. And they will take the bird's feet and beard, and leave the carcass to predators. Since the drumsticks and wings are tough and stringy, about the only useful purpose this meat serves is when boiled for flavor in stews, soups or turkey stock.

If the turkey is plucked, it can be smoked on a water smoker, like Coleman's Cookin' Machine, which allows for either water or charcoal smoking. Many hunters think that a bird cooked on a water smoker is the most flavorful way to prepare a bird for the table. The important key is that the bird be plucked and not skinned. Any time a bird is skinned, the meat tends to dry out rapidly, become tough and lose much of its flavor.

Here are several recipes that will tickle the taste buds of even the most persnickety gourmet.

Roast Wild Turkey

10 lb. wild turkey
  salt and pepper
1 onion, chopped
1 lb. pork sausage
1½ quarts soft breadcrumbs
  ¼ tsp. pepper
2 tsp. salt
3 T. parsley
  bacon
  bacon fat

Dress turkey and weigh to determine cooking time. Season with salt and pepper inside and out. Make stuffing. Cook onion with sausage in skillet for five minutes, and then add remaining ingredients except bacon. Moisten with a little hot water if too dry.

Place turkey breast down in uncovered pan and stuff. Bake at 350 degrees for a total of 20 to 25 minutes per pound. Roast for half the total required time, then turn bird breast up.

Lay strips of bacon over breast or cover with piece of cloth dipped in bacon fat. Finish roasting. If cloth is used, remove it after cooking if a deeper brown is desired.

Test by pushing a sharp-tined fork into a thigh and the thick of the breast. If the fork enters easily and if the juice has no red tint, the bird is ready.

Turkey & Rice Casserole

  3 cups turkey, cooked and diced
  1 cup celery, diced
  ½ cup onion, diced
  1 cup cooked brown or wild rice
  ¾ cup mayonnaise
  1 can cream of chicken soup
  1 10 oz. pkg. cheddar cheese
  salt and pepper

Mix together. Top with croutons or chips. Bake at 350 degrees for 45 minutes, uncovered.

Turkey Tetrazzini
   2 cups cooked turkey, cut in small pieces
   ½ lb. fresh mushrooms, thinly sliced
      butter
   ½ lb. spaghetti
   2 T. butter
   2 T. flour
   2 cups hot turkey or chicken broth
   1 cup rich cream
   2 T. dry sherry
      salt and pepper to taste
      Parmesan cheese

Prepare turkey. Saute mushrooms in butter until browned. Prepare spaghetti according to package directions, using salted water. Make a cream sauce by blending butter and flour; gradually adding hot broth. When this mixture reaches boiling point, reduce heat and add the cream, sherry, salt and pepper to taste.

Divide the sauce in half. Add the turkey and mushrooms to half of the sauce, the spaghetti to the other half. Press the spaghetti mixture into a ring shape in a well-greased casserole. Place the turkey and mushroom mixture in center. Cover with cheese. Bake, uncovered, at 325 degrees until brown.

Smoked Turkey On Covered Grill
   1 turkey breast
   1 sm. bottle vinegar
      handful of salt
   1 bag charcoal
   1 bag hickory chips
      charcoal lighter
      bucket of water

Rub turkey all over with salt. Pour vinegar over entire turkey breast. Cover for about one hour. Light fire, using only a handful of charcoal. Soak chips in water to be added as you cook. Put turkey on grill on its back with cavity filled with vinegar. Turn every two hours. Cook a total of five to seven hours. Add a few lumps of charcoal occasionally. Add chips to keep smoke going.

Turkey Pie

1 nine-inch pie shell, baked
2 cups cooked, cubed turkey
1 cup chopped celery
⅓ cup chopped green pepper
2 T. finely chopped onions
½ cup coarsely chopped pecans
¼ tsp. pepper
½ tsp salt
1 T. lemon juice
½ cup mayonnaise
1 10¾ ounce can cream of chicken soup
½ cup Swiss or Cheddar cheese, shredded
3 T. snipped fresh parsley

Combine turkey, celery, green pepper, onion, pecans, pepper, salt, lemon juice, mayonnaise and soup. Spoon into pie shell. Sprinkle cheese and parsley over top. Bake in a 350-degree oven for 30 minutes or until heated through. Sprinkle with chopped pecans.

Grandmother Murdock's Turkey Dressing

2 cups chopped onion
2 cups celery, chopped
5 cups cornbread, crumbled
5 cups Bisquick
1 tsp. sage
1 tsp. salt
6 eggs, well beaten
5 cups turkey or chicken broth or enough to soak
  ingredients well

Cook onion and celery in enough stock to make tender. Mix all ingredients with stock and place in greased pan. Bake in oven at 350 degrees for one hour until brown. Serve with gravy.

20

The Turkey And
The New York Lady

Priscilla introduced herself while we were both hunting the Loch Ness monster in Scotland. Unlike turkey hunting, a monster hunt is conducted in nice clothes at civilized times of the day. People attracted by a monster hunt have a great curiosity along with some degree of insanity. Otherwise they'd be like all the other skeptics and non-believers who never go in search of adventure or the unknown.

Turkey hunters also love adventure. They will go into unknown swamps, woods, and deserts, and climb high mountains to hunt a gobbling bird. So when I first met this New York Lady on a monster hunt, I knew she had the potential to be a turkey chaser.

Realize first of all that people who live in New York, and I'm talking downtown Manhattan, are different from most other folks in the world. They must be to live and work shoulder to shoulder with so many other individuals. The only critters I know who enjoy living that close together besides New Yorkers are martins, better known by city dwellers as swallows. If you've ever seen a colony of martins all living together in 10 or 15 gourd houses, you know what I mean.

After meeting Priscilla, it's obvious that New York ladies are different from southern ladies. It's also obvious that New York women don't like being called ladies. They view the term, ''lady'' as an insult. In my home state of Alabama, however, the term commands the utmost respect.

You would assume that people who live in the world's communication center would understand how to communicate with people from other lands, cultures and backgrounds. But when I called Priscilla, "Miss Priscilla," boy did she get her hackles up! In the South, putting the word, "Miss," in front of a lady's first name is a term of respect. Whether she's married is irrelevant; you use the term "Miss" to show that you respect her.

However for New York ladies, using the title of "Miss," is interpreted as a put-down or, as Priscilla told me later, "Sounds as though you're talking down to a woman like you would talk down to a child or anyone else you feel is beneath you."

After settling these regional preferences, we discovered we had many things in common. Basically, we both worked in the print media. We also found that we loved adventure. When we talked about our favorite things to do, I told Priscilla about turkey hunting. She seemed fascinated by the lure of the wild and the way a hunter had to talk to a turkey to get a gobbler to come in for a shot. Since she was so interested, I invited her to come "down home" to Alabama for a turkey hunt with my family in the spring. Much to my surprise, she agreed to leave her family for a few days and come South. So the date was set.

When you take a New Yorker on a down-home turkey hunt, you have a moral responsibility to do everything within your powers to ensure success. Therefore I called my good friends, Dr. John Lanier and Leo Allen, owners and operators of Bent Creek Lodge in Jachin, Alabama, and asked if they would mind if Priscilla and I came to hunt the 22,000 acres they control.

John Lanier said, "Bring her on down. We've got a turkey or two she can chase."

I quickly realized there are some things to consider when you guide an asphalt jungler in the woods to take a turkey. Asphalt junglers are accustomed to concrete, plate glass windows, traffic lights, smog, muggings, fast walking, subways and a completely different lifestyle than the dirt road sports who hunt gobblers. Most New Yorkers have never seen a suit of camo—except on the 6:00 p.m. news when they watch reports of wars going on all over the world.

So I told Priscilla, "Don't worry about your clothes. Just bring a pair of snow boots that are good for walking. Make sure those boots are not red or white. I'll take care of your clothing."

Although asphalt junglers understand what snow boots are, some probably are uninformed on the subject of hunting boots. Therefore to talk to them, you must use terminology they can interpret. Priscilla informed me that she had a pair of green riding boots that she had worn on a recent trip down the Amazon River and to the Galapagos Islands. She felt sure they would be appropriate. That information told me that unlike many city slickers, Priscilla had slid off of the asphalt a time or two and had the potential to develop into a turkey hunter.

Then I mentioned to her that I didn't understand how anybody could live in New York City for long without a good airing out. "Miss Priscilla, I don't believe that the Good Lord intended for so many people to live so close together without occasionally getting out in the woods and on the water to clear all the corruption out of their minds that comes from living in such compact communities."

Priscilla didn't take offense. The following spring she mounted the worldwide commuter's bus in the sky and flew from the asphalt jungles of New York City to the mecca of dirt road sports in Alabama. We drove to Bent Creek Lodge that night, and I outfitted her in camouflage.

Priscilla was provided with a complete camo outfit. A headnet and gloves completed her ensemble.

Before daylight, we were taken by Lanier and Allen to the area we were to hunt.

"Walk up this little woods road, and you'll come to a clear cut," Lanier instructed. "Since there's been two or three turkey gobbling around that clear cut, you should be able to slip up on one."

So before daylight we left the truck to slip down the road, stopping occasionally for me to hoot like a barred owl. I could tell by the twinkle in her eye that she was wondering what kind of a nut she was with in the woods. After all, she'd probably never heard an owl hoot in New York, much less seen a human trying to make owl sounds.

We talked about how hooting like an owl would make a turkey shock gobble. She looked as though she understood what I was saying. But by using the vocabulary of a turkey hunter when talking to an asphalt jungler, the result was more like a plumber listening to a nuclear physicist.

We heard several toms gobble, attempted to set up on two or three different birds, saw a couple of turkey and got lost in the unfamiliar woods twice. By two in the afternoon, I could see that her enthusiasm for gobbler chasing was waning. So we headed back to the lodge for lunch and a much needed break.

"What do you think about us hunting those turkey in the field behind your veterinarian clinic?" I asked Lanier at lunch. There was always a good flock in the big pasture behind Lanier's office. But as Lanier explained, "You can hunt those turkey, John, but you probably won't kill one. Those birds just won't work well to a call since several folks have fooled with them. Although you can see them, you have a slim chance of killing one. I'd suggest going back behind the lodge itself and finding a turkey in those fields. But go ahead and hunt anywhere on the property you want."

First, we went behind the lodge and spotted six hens in the first field. Belly crawling to the edge of the field, I let Priscilla look at the birds with binoculars. Although we checked eight more fields and called several times, we didn't see another turkey. The afternoon was fast slipping away as was Priscilla's excitement for the hunt, since we had already walked about ten miles that day. I was concerned too with my inability to find and work a bird, and wanted her to see a longbeard up close.

So with about 1½ hours of daylight left, we went down to Lanier's animal clinic to check whether or not there were any gobblers in the clinic's fields. When we circled around behind the building, I spotted three big gobblers close to the wood's edge. They were mature gobblers and only about 350 yards away.

Priscilla decided to try for one.

We loaded our shotguns, and went back to the paved road in front of the clinic. Running about 150 yards down the road, we came to a ditch and a fenceline that had grown up in briars. We climbed into the ditch and slipped up the fenceline. There was a rolling hill between us and the turkey. By staying in the ditch and under the lip of the hill, we were able to move rapidly and unnoticed for 300 yards.

Then we entered the pine forest on the back side of the field without seeing the turkey or them seeing us. Moving swiftly through the woods, we stayed about 50 yards from the edge of the field. We quietly made our way to the edge. There was one lone gobbler about 100 yards away. Walking back into the woods, we circled through the forest hoping to come up on the edge of the field directly behind the turkey.

While standing in the woods, we spotted the turkey. He was right in front of us. The only way to get to the edge of the field without the gobbler seeing us was to make a long, slow belly crawl.

Lying on our stomachs, we inched along like a worm on the ground that sees a robin overhead. As we crawled, I searched for a big tree where we could sit and call a gobbler. Then we spotted a large pine about 20 yards from the edge of the field. As we moved through the woods, I was surprised at how quietly Priscilla was crawling. She had become woods-wise quickly, not talking but paying close attention and listening to the sounds in the woods. Now the supreme test was before us.

When we finally arrived at the big pine, the gobbler was 70 yards away. I was surprised we had crawled that close without spooking him.

Using binoculars we again checked the lone bird. He had an eight-inch beard, and he was still feeding in the field. I got out my calls and prepared to talk to the tom. But before I could start calling, he turned and headed in our direction!

"Aren't you going to call?" Priscilla whispered.

"Not yet," I said. If he keeps walking in this direction, you'll get your shot."

The turkey changed course slightly. We responded by sliding around the tree. The old gobbler was steadily pecking and walking toward us when I whispered, "The turkey's at 50 yards now. Go ahead and take the safety off of your gun. Put your cheek on the stock, start looking down the barrel and see the bead. When the bird gets close enough, place that bead on the turkey's neck where the feathers join the head. Then squeeze the trigger. I'll tell you when to shoot."

She followed these instructions and the ones we had discussed before. The gobbler was performing just as he should.

"He's at 30 yards. You can shoot him now, but let him get as close as he will. Remember to feel the stock of the gun against your cheek, look straight down the barrel and put the bead on the turkey's neck."

Priscilla began to breathe harder. I was afraid she might hyperventilate, and tried to calm her down by telling her to wait and relax. The huge bird closed the distance and headed straight toward us. The hunt was too perfect. Almost too perfect. That bothered me, so in anticipation of a problem, I slowly raised my gun to my knee. Her breathing was heavy as the large tom came closer.

"Fifteen yards. Keep that bead on his neck."

We could see the gobbler's eyelashes. The big beard on his chest swayed back and forth as he walked closer. He had a fine set of spurs.

The turkey came to a three-strand barbed wire fence that was 12 yards in front of us and ducked under the wire. Now the bird was at about 10 steps and looked like a giant potentate in all his splendor.

The moment of truth was at hand.

"Shoot," I whispered.

The gun failed to report. Again I whispered, "Shoot."

I took inventory. Everything was right. Priscilla's head was down, her finger was on the trigger and the barrel was pointed directly at the turkey's head. All she had to do was squeeze the trigger. However, the gun didn't go off.

Now the bird had his neck straight up, having heard Priscilla's labored breathing and my whispering. Finally I implored, "Priscilla, shoot the turkey, please."

That gobbler may have been old, but he wasn't deaf. He heard me, putted three times, turned around, ducked under the fence and started off at a quick trot. Realizing that Priscilla wasn't going to shoot, I swung to the bird and let the Winchester three-inch magnum do the job it was designed to do. The bird tumbled. I hopped up, vaulted the fence and dashed to the bird. Immediately I put my foot on the longbeard's head. In short order Priscilla was right behind me.

"Why didn't you shoot?" I asked.

"I don't know," she answered. "I was so excited and breathing so hard I couldn't hear you. I was concentrating so much on staying still that I just didn't shoot. I don't understand what happened. I just couldn't believe that the turkey was coming straight to us. And then there he was, right in front of us."

We both began to babble in the excitement and enthusiasm associated with taking a giant gobbler.

"I really don't care who squeezed the trigger," she said. "We got our turkey, and that was one of the most exciting things I've ever done."

With big smiles on our faces and a gobbler over one shoulder, we headed back to the clubhouse.

21

It Doesn't Get
Any Better Than This

There are some people who are just enjoyable to be around. They can tell a good story, enjoy the outdoor experience and talk about anything from the world's economy to which kind of camo is best for turkey hunting. These people's lives are made up of the mundane, everyday things like getting up, going to work, reading a daily newspaper, cutting the grass on Saturday and going to church on Sunday. But they also love high adventure, new challenges and the sport of chasing gobblers. They're people like the Stephenses of Birmingham, Alabama—Elton B., his sons, Jim and Elton B., Jr., and his son-in-law, Dixon Brooke.

Although I had fished with these folks several times before, our first turkey hunt together was the most exciting experience of all. Mr. Elton B. had arranged for each of us to have a guide and hunt different lands near Ft. Deposit, Alabama. This was one of the greatest hunts of my life, and I'll remember and cherish the memory of it until some minimum wage worker throws dirt in my face when I'm looking up from a six-foot deep hole.

We got up before daylight and had a light breakfast. My guide for the day was a young man named Bob. Although Bob had been hunting turkey for a couple of years he had never hunted this property.

As we drove into the woods, the road was red and very muddy. About three miles back in the forest, there was a low spot that lead to a red clay hill. As we hit the mud, the ground seemed to sink when the truck started up the hill. Halfway up, the tires spun, the truck sank and the frame of the vehicle became firmly lodged against the hill. The truck was stuck.

When a disaster like this strikes, the mettle of a man is tested. Some outdoorsmen would have screamed, hollered, cussed, spit, stomped and kicked the tires on the truck. That behavior is justified to relieve frustration and aggravation. But Bob was cut from a different cloth.

"Well, we're stuck," the mild-mannered young man announced. "So we might as well go hunting. We can't do anything about it until later on in the morning anyway. Let's not allow this to ruin our hunt."

I realized then that I was in the company of one of God's noblest creatures, a man who could ...

... soar above disaster.

... continue on with his daily routine.

... leave his problems behind.

... go on with the more important business of life —like turkey hunting.

We have all been with such men before. He's someone who, after chasing a gobbler all morning, says...

..."Well, I'm already late for work. We may as well hunt the rest of the day."

... "I was supposed to take my wife shopping, but since I'm late, she's going to be mad anyway. Guess I might as well hunt."

... "I was supposed to plow that big field out back today, and rain is expected for tomorrow. But turkey season only comes once a year, and there'll be plenty of days to plow."

So when Bob was willing to leave his truck stuck in the mud and not let it interfere with his turkey hunting, he demonstrated poise and character not found in many men, even ardent outdoorsmen. We walked about a half a mile when we came to a crest of a hill and listened for a turkey to gobble. I hooted like an owl. Two gobblers fired back.

"There's one turkey in that bottom and another on that next hill," I told Bob. "I'll move toward the turkey in the bottom, and you try and get the turkey on the hill."

Bob looked up at me with a surprised face as he said, "I'm supposed to guide you, Mr. Phillips. So we'll go to whichever turkey you want to take, and I'll call for you."

I quickly explained to Bob that my daddy was the only Mr. Phillips I knew and that I was simply, John.

"Look," I said. "Wouldn't you rather kill your own turkey? Since we've got two birds gobbling, we may be able to bag two toms and be out of here before 8:00 a.m."

Bob agreed that he would rather hunt than guide but assured me that his number one purpose for being there was to help me kill a turkey. He in no way wanted to interfere with my hunt or cause me to not be successful.

"O.K., Bob, here's the deal," I told him. "You go after the turkey on the hill, and I'll try for the turkey in the bottom. If we fail to get a bird, we'll meet on the road in the bottom in about 1½ hours. But while these toms are gobbling, we ought to go after them."

Bob trotted across the bottom and up to the next ridge. I went off the hill into a little valley and began to head in the direction where I had heard the turkey. I owl hooted again, and the turkey gobbled. I hesitated because there was a small creek in front of me. I tried to decide whether the turkey was on my side or the other side of the creek. I owl hooted once more. When the turkey gobbled back, I decided to cross the creek.

Sitting beside a large water oak, I took out a Lynch Foolproof box call and yelped to the turkey. The tom gobbled. I laid the box down and picked up Knight and Hale's pushbutton call that had been given to me as a present the week before. I hadn't even had a chance to test this new call on a bird. But since I had a gobbling turkey 75-100 yards in front of me, I thought I would give the little pushbutton a chance.

By pushing and pulling the dial on the lightweight call, the box yelped. The turkey answered. Although I enjoy playing with calls, I'd rather harvest a turkey. I could tell by his call that he was closer than before. So I laid my call down, picked up my shotgun and prepared for action.

In less than 10 minutes, I heard the turkey walking. When I saw the gobbler, he was at 30 yards. But there were some small bushes between me and the turkey. I looked in the direction the turkey was walking and spotted a small opening about 25 yards from where I was sitting. I turned to face the opening, put my Remington 1187 SP on my knee, and waited for the bird.

As the turkey moved into the opening, he stuck his neck up, and I squeezed the trigger. He went down. I packed the bird out to the road, and in a few minutes Bob appeared.

"What kind of call were you using?" Bob asked. "The turkey I was hunting flew down off the roost and went running straight for you. I bet you killed the turkey I went after and not the gobbler you originally were hunting. I've never seen a turkey run to a call like that."

Bob's explanation made sense, since the turkey had come from the direction in which Bob had gone. And the turkey I went after did sound much farther away than the one I had bagged.

"We've still got plenty of morning left," I told Bob. "Since I've already got my turkey, why don't we team up on a tom and see if we can get you one? I'll call, and you shoot."

The plan suited Bob. We soon found another tom gobbling. I put Bob about 30 yards in front of me and started to call. When the turkey answered, I felt sure Bob would get a shot. But instead of moving straight in, the turkey circled and came in behind us. I could hear him walking behind me, however, I couldn't communicate to Bob to turn around and face me so he could see the turkey. Finally that tom walked off.

As the morning wore on, we had the chance to call two more birds. But one turkey was across water, and we couldn't reach him. The other gobbler was on the wrong side of a big thicket we couldn't get around. Therefore, about 10:00 a.m. we gave up our hunt to try and get the truck out of the mud.

Bob went to a nearby farmhouse and called a wrecker that came out into the woods and pulled out the truck.

When we arrived back at the camp, Mr. Elton B. was already in camp, Jim had seen a couple of turkey but didn't have a shot, and Dixon had missed a gobbler. Elton B., Jr. was still out hunting. After we had waited for 45 minutes or so, we decided to return to the place where Bob and I had hunted. I would guide Dixon and Jim since Bob had to be at work. Mr. Elton B. could go with his guide, William Johnson.

We went to the woods where Bob and I had hunted that morning. However, we stopped before we got to the hill. I showed Mr. Elton B. and Johnson where I'd heard the turkey in the bottom. Then Jim, Dixon and I headed deeper into the woods.

"OK, if we're going to attempt to bag a tom in the middle of the day, we're going to to have to run-and-gun," I said. "If we hear a turkey gobble, we'll have to attempt to reach him quickly and then set up fast to take him."

Jim and Dixon nodded yes. After we'd walked about one-half

mile, we came to a high ridge, and I owl hooted. Since a turkey gobbled back, I urged, "Let's go."

We left the ridge on a dead run with me in front and Jim and Dixon right on my heels. After running about 50-60 yards and just starting up a hill, I saw a sight that caused me to throw my feet straight out in front of me and land flat on my back. I hit the ground like one of those movie cowboys who gets lassoed by the villain who's standing on the ground with his rope tied to a tree.

After I fell on my back, I began waving my hands toward the side of the road to let Jim and Dixon know that they needed to get off the road and hide. Just as I had crested the hill, I had seen the fanned tails of three strutting gobblers that were looking away from me. I hoped they hadn't seen or heard my fall.

Very quietly, I slid on my back to the edge of the road and off the side of the bank beside the road. Jim was lying in a ditch belly down on the other side of the road, and Dixon was about 20 yards behind me.

After I had given everyone a chance to settle down, I made some light clucks and purrs to which the gobblers answered. In a few short minutes, the three toms began to march up the road like soldiers in a procession. The turkey were closing now, and when they were 30 yards from Jim and about 20 yards from me, I began to scream, "Shoot!" in my mind.

One of the most difficult tasks in buddy hunting is communicating with the other hunter without speaking or moving. So as hard as I knew how, I concentrated and shouted with my mind, "Shoot!" But Jim never squeezed the trigger.

Later Jim told me that he thought the turkey were just out of range. He hated to shoot and possibly miss or spook the birds or even worse, wound one. I agreed that if Jim was unsure of the distance that he did the right thing by not shooting. However, this still did not solve the problem of three longbeard turkey standing 20 yards in front of me in the middle of the road.

Well, Dixon probably couldn't see the birds, because he was a little below me on the bank. Since I'd already taken a bird that morning, I'd left my shotgun at the camp and had no intentions of trying to take a gobbler. However, when the turkey came across the road to the side where Dixon and I were, they stood right in front of us. I could watch them breathe. In my frustration I looked all around for a rock to toss at them.

The toms moved off to my right, where I assumed Dixon could see them. Then I was mentally screaming, "Shoot, Dixon, shoot!"

But the sound of a reporting shotgun never came. The birds started to walk off, and I called them back. Again, Dixon failed to fire. This time, however, the gobblers went off to my right directly toward Dixon and passed within about 20 yards of him. As I watched the birds walk off, I kept waiting for the shot that never came.

After a few more minutes, I called once more. The turkey returned! Still Dixon didn't shoot.

Finally the three longbeards had had about enough of the game and walked away from us down the side of the road. When they were well out of sight behind the hill, the three of us called a meeting in the middle of the road. That's when Jim explained that he thought the turkey were too far from him, which was why he didn't take a shot. Dixon said that even though he could watch the turkey moving part of the time, he never had a clear head shot.

So we laid a new strategy. We assumed that since we hadn't spooked them, the birds would think that the way they had walked by us was safe. So if they confronted danger farther down the road, they might return the same way they had left.

So Jim and I left Dixon behind on the side of the road as a sentinel to ambush the gobblers if we spooked them. Then we took off at a fast pace on the opposite side of the road from where the turkey were walking, made a big circle to get in front of them, and sat down just below the crest of a hill beside a big pine tree.

We figured that if the turkey would work to a different call that they should come up over the crest of that hill. Then when Jim saw the birds, they would be within easy killing range and he should be able to bag a gobbler. Jim and I sat shoulder to shoulder as I called. Immediately one of the toms fired back a gobble. We could hear the birds off in the distance.

"Get ready, Jim. You're going to kill a turkey."

Although the big gobblers had made fools of us the first time around, we'd have our day in the sun. Some time passed before I called again. This time when one of the toms answered back, We could hear him strutting and drumming just over the hill.

"We're going to get a turkey," I said.

But instead of coming straight to us, the turkey walked off to our right. Apparently they planned to circle us before they came in to where we were. So we slid around the tree and got into position to bag the gobblers. We let the woods settle for about five minutes and then started calling once more. The birds gobbled and appeared about 60 yards away on top of a hill. I told Jim once more to get ready. Jim had his shotgun on his knee, he was in a good shooting position and the birds were on their way.

I was beginning to swell with pride. I had already taken a gobbler at daylight, found these three in the middle of the road, and called them up three times to within 20 yards of us. This fourth and final time, I'd be able to call them to where Jim could take one. I was smugly thinking, "Life doesn't get any better than this."

However, if you've ever been on a roll on a crap table, you know that no matter how good it gets or how much money you've won, sooner or later you'll crap out. But as the turkey approached, I could see no way we could fail, except ...

Why hadn't I seen it before? If I'd only spotted it before the turkey had come around the hill we could have moved and gotten in front of the large, fallen pine tree lying directly between the turkey and us at about 35 yards.

I knew from experience that when the turkey arrived at that tree they would stop, hang up and look for the hen they thought had been calling. We were in a fairly clean pine forest, and the old gobblers knew they should be able to see that hen when they reached that tree. I realized that if they didn't spot the hen when they reached that fallen pine, they would leave.

"The turkey will stop at that downed pine tree," I whispered. "When they pause, I'll yelp one time loud to get the birds to stick up their heads. If any of the toms puts his head above that pine, then shoot. If you don't take him I don't think we'll get another shot."

As expected, the turkey walked to the big downed pine and hung up.

"Ready, Jim?" I asked.

Jim hunkered down on his gun, ready to make the shot. Most of their bodies were out of sight. But when I yelped, one of the gobblers stuck his head up, and Jim fired. However, as quickly as the turkey's head came up, it went back down. All three gobblers broke and ran.

The turkey were gone, and we could tell from the direction they were running that they weren't going back toward Dixon. Sure we didn't bag a bird that day, but we had had a great hunt...

... We had worked those toms in close, real close, four times.

... I had bagged a bird at daylight.

... Jim, Dixon and I had shared one of the finest days of turkey hunting that I'd ever experienced.

That's what turkey hunting is about: Having the opportunity to call gobblers, working them in close and having good friends with whom to share the experience.

22

Birds Of The Same Feather

Outdoor writers are weird, strange people. Normal society rejects the thought of anyone earning a living by hunting, fishing, camping, hiking, canoeing and enjoying the outdoors. When you mention outdoor activities in the same paragraph with the word, "work," most people's minds come out of gear. A red light goes on that flashes, "Does Not Compute."

But I learned many years ago that work doesn't have to be miserable to be defined as work. There are some individuals who've learned the joy of work and who arise every morning with eager anticipation of going to their jobs. However, these are rare people. In the work-a-day world where we live, folks who refer to work as an honor are said to be strange, like outdoor writers.

I enjoy the company of fellow scribes, who understand that besides hunting, fishing and taking pictures an outdoor writer must spend time sliding a pencil across a paper or beating the keys of a computer until his fingers lose their sensitivity. Although outdoor journalism is an exciting vocation, many times it is a lonely sojourn into one's own mind to reflect on and capture the essence of the wild, which often involves more than landing a big bass or taking a large tom.

Every outdoor writer is different. Not all have done everything that every other outdoor writer has done. Such was the case of Dave Richey from Buckley, Michigan. Dave is an outdoor writer who has bagged bear, moose, antelope, mule deer and whitetail. Richey has one of the most well-rounded outdoor educations of any man I know.

But Richey had never been turkey hunting until he came to Bent Creek Lodge near Jachin, Alabama. He intended to hunt with Harold Knight and David Hale of Knight and Hale Game Calls. Richey's wife, Kay, had accompanied Richey on the hunt. As luck would have it, my son, John, and I were in camp at the same time.

John and Harold Knight are hunting buddies, ever since Knight took John on his first successful turkey hunt. The two wanted to hunt together once more during our stay at Bent Creek. That meant that Richey would be without a guide, since Hale was guiding Kay Richey. So I volunteered to take Dave Richey.

The object of the hunt was to get Richey a turkey. But being the kind of friend and hunter he is, Richey told me, "Look, John, I came to Alabama to get a story on turkey hunting. I don't have to kill a turkey. If you get a chance to take a tom, shoot him. We need a turkey to photograph, and I must have an adventure to write about. So whether you or I kill the turkey doesn't really matter to me. I've just got to get a story about turkey hunting."

And that's the way most professional outdoor writers are: the story comes first and their own recreation second. Richey and I entered the woods before daylight. As soon as we climbed out of the truck, we heard a turkey gobble about 125 yards away in the woods. We slipped into the woods and set up to call the bird. Although the tom would answer us, he wouldn't come to where we were. Since this was my first time in this part of Bent Creek's woods, I didn't know where I was or where the turkey was located. But because the gobbler talked back to me when I called to him, I felt we should be able to bag the bird.

However, after 45 minutes of having the turkey hung up and not coming to us, I realized that we would have to circle the turkey and find another place to call to him. As we made our circle, we hit a small stream, which apparently was what had caused the turkey to hang up. The gobbler probably just didn't want to cross the creek.

So we got on the same side of the creek as the turkey. After letting the woods settle for about 15-20 minutes, we called again. The tom must have flown across the creek, because when he answered, he was on the other side of the creek from us, walking away toward the spot we had left.

Richey and I made another move back to where we had been

originally. But we never caught up to that turkey. However, I wasn't too concerned since we had heard two or three more toms gobble that morning. I felt that we had plenty of birds to work.

Eventually we chased turkey all over the hills and hollows of that particular woodlot until about 10:30 a.m. Each time we'd call to a bird, the tom wouldn't come. Later when we would investigate, we would find that either there was a thicket or a creek between us and the gobbler, or that hens had reached the bronze baron before he could get to us.

Although we had worked toms all morning long, we still had failed to bag a bird. So at 10:30 a.m., Richey and I tried to walk out of the woods. "Tried," is an appropriate term, because we were lost. I remembered what an old friend told me when he was turned around in a swamp on a cloudy day, "I may be lost in the woods, but I'm not lost from the house." Richey and I could hear traffic on two roads in the distance.

We knew that eventually we would return to our pick up point. But how long that "eventually" might take was of some concern to both of us. I had made the classic mistake of being so intent on chasing gobblers and trying to get Richey a turkey that I hadn't taken note of the woods as we passed through them or considered how to come out of them when the hunt was over. But Richey and I were having a good time. About every 10 minutes I would call, hoping to get lucky. At 11:00 a.m., deep in the woods, I called and heard a hen cutting.

"That's an excited hen," I said. "There must be a gobbler close by. She must be on the other side of this small creek. Let's cross the creek, set up, see if we can call to her and maybe make a turkey gobble."

We crossed the creek and sat shoulder to shoulder by a large hickory tree. I started calling, and immediately a gobbler answered back. But since I also could hear hens talking, I knew the gobbler was with hens. I called once more, and the tom gobbled again, which let me know that at least he was interested, even if he did have some lady friends.

I planned my strategy. In the early part of the season, I had been guilty of calling too much to gobbling turkey. Consequently, I didn't bag some birds I should have. This tom already had hens with him. So I decided to try some coy hen tactics. I let the turkey gobble and wouldn't answer him for about 10 minutes. Then I gave some soft clucks and whines to tell the gobbler that I was still in the area but totally unimpressed with his gobbling and the harem of hens he had with him.

The next time I called, he gobbled back. Another gobbler, about 100 yards past the first tom, answered. I explained what was happening.

"Dave, the first gobbler is with his hens, and the second tom is talking to me too. The second turkey may come running in, hoping to get to us and pick us up before the first tom reaches us. So we may have the chance to take two gobblers instead of one. Get ready to shoot."

Before I could call again, I heard the first gobbler strutting and drumming as well as a hen giving soft calls off to my left. At the same time, the second tom gobbled. Right after his gobble, I heard another hunter in the distance using a box call trying to call to the same turkey.

"Wow," I thought, "We've really got a hunt going. There's a gobbler with hens strutting and drumming. Another tom is gobbling at the bird with the hens. I'm attempting to work both toms, and there's another hunter just over the next hill calling the same turkey. I don't know what will be the outcome, but Dave is certainly going to get an exciting story."

My mind was brought back into the hunt when off to my left I saw a patch of white moving through the woods. As I began to strain my eyes and slowly move my head so as not to spook the turkey, I could see the giant gobbler coming toward us in a full strut with a hen right by his side. The bird was about 70 yards from us when I whispered to Richey, who was sitting on my right, "The turkey is coming up to my left."

Richey whispered back in a low voice, "John, we've been hunting turkey all morning long. If you get a shot at that bird, take him."

I said nothing but watched the bird intently. The gobbler kept coming. When he stepped behind a tree, I put my gun on my knee and aimed. Although I wanted Richey to bag the tom, he was right. We'd walked too far, hunted too hard and been lost too long to let a longbeard get away. But I also remembered that Richey was the hunter. I was the guide. If there was any way to let Richey kill the gobbler, I meant to do it.

When the gobbler was at 30 yards, within easy killing distance, the second tom gobbled. The big turkey by us turned away from us and started walking toward his rival.

"Dave, I'm afraid the turkey is leaving us," I whispered. Let's try one more tactic to put the bird in front of you.''

I'd been using a box call to bring in the bird. But I always keep a diaphragm call in my mouth during turkey season. Several nights I've almost fallen asleep with this call in my mouth. I realized that the bird was too close for me to pick up the box and talk to him. So as quietly as I could, I gave some soft yelps on the mouth diaphragm call. The gobbler that had been walking off in a full strut, dropped his strut, began to turn parallel to us, and started quartering to us.

"Dave, you're going to get to shoot the turkey," I whispered. "He's within range. When he steps out from behind those trees, aim for where the head joins the neck and shoot him.''

The big bird walked out from behind the tree, and Richey nailed him. Practically before the smoke had finished coming out of Richey's barrel, he lowered his gun and I jumped up and ran to the turkey. I had already mentioned to Richey what I would do when he shot the bird. I knew that because he was a professional outdoorsman he was well-acquainted with what to do with a firearm.

As soon as I jumped up, I saw Richey swinging his gun away from the bird. I sprinted like a cat being chased by a bulldog to where the gobbler lay. I put my foot on the turkey's head and grabbed his feet. In less than a heartbeat, Richey was standing beside me as I breathed heavily from the sprint and the excitement of having helped a friend get his first bird.

"Hey, John, you better slow down. You're going to have a heart attack," Richey said to me. "You're getting too excited.''

As I grinned back at Richey, I explained, "Dave, when I don't get this excited over taking a turkey, I'll give up turkey hunting and outdoor writing and start selling insurance.''

Glossary

Beard. Hair-like growths made of feathers that protrude from both hens' and gobblers' chests. The beard, however, is usually a primary sexual characteristic of the male. Beginning growth from the breast of young gobblers around the age of five months, beards generally grow at the rate of four to five inches per year.

Box call. A thin-walled wooden box with a wooden paddle lid attached to one end of the box. By sliding the paddle lid across the open edge of the box, the instrument can be played to make most of the calls of the wild turkey. To produce the proper sound, the lid of the box as well as the two sides of the box are usually chalked.

Cackling. An excited call given by the hen turkey that is made up of a series of fast yelps.

Calling. Noises and sounds made by the hunter to try and lure a gobbler to within gun range. Calling is not just the use of hen or gobbler sounds. Owl, crow and hawk calls are also used.

Calling, raspy. A coarse sounding call that a hen makes that sounds as though she has laryngitis.

Calling, sweet. A smooth, clear, crisp, healthy sounding call.

Call-shy. A term that describes a turkey that probably has been called to, shot at and spooked by hunters.

Cedar box with striker. A cedar box call, similar to the box and paddle box call with which most hunters are familiar. Instead of having a paddle for the lid of the box call, the hunter has some type of striker that he holds in his hand and passes across the lid.

Chufa. A grass that has nut-like roots which turkeys like to eat.

Cluck. A hen turkey's sound that is much like a woman talking to herself, including contented and excited clucks.

Controlled burning. The act of setting fire to the woods to burn away vegetation and release the nutrients in the soil. Results in new growth of young plants without damaging or destroying the timber. Controlled burning is a key management tool for wild turkey production.

Crow call. The sounds that crows make when they notify one another of their positions. The crow call is used by turkey hunters to cause a tom to shock gobble.

Cutting. Very fast, loud stutter yelps and clucks much like the beginning of a cackle, but not going all the way through a cackle.

Decoy. An artificial reproduction of a hen turkey

Diaphragm caller. A call made of tape, lead, and latex rubber that is inserted into the roof of the hunter's mouth. Turkey sounds are produced when the hunter blows air over the call.

Displaying. A turkey strutting.

Dominant gobbler. The dominant gobbler in a flock who is at the top in the pecking order of the birds. Most often determined by strength, size, age and intelligence.

Dominant hen. Similar to the gobbler. The dominant hen is the female boss of the flock and may determine where the flock will go.

Double calling. Two hunters purposefully calling at the same time to imitate more than one turkey in the same area.

Droppings. Turkey excretion in a stool form.

Dropping, gobbler. A turkey stool that has the shape of a fish hook or a question mark.

Dropping, hen. A stool that is round and resembles a small cow dropping.

Drumming. The sound a tom turkey makes when he struts.

Eastern wild turkey. (Meleagris gallopavo silvestris) One of six subspecies of North American wild turkey that is found mainly in the eastern U.S.

Fly up/fly down cackle. An excited call that the hen turkey makes when she jumps off the limb in the morning and flies down to the ground to greet a new day. Also made when she jumps off the ground to fly into a tree for a night's rest.

Friction call. Any type of call where two objects are rubbed against each other to produce the sounds that turkey make, including a slate and box call.

Gobble. The sound that a wild turkey makes that gives away his location, calls hens to mate and notifies other turkey that he is in the area.

Gobbler. A male turkey.

Hawk call. The sound that a hawk makes as it flies overhead. Used by turkey hunters to cause turkey to shock gobble.

Hen. A female turkey.

Hung-up. A turkey that stops a certain distance from the hunter just out of gun range and refuses to come any closer.

Intergrade mixture. Turkey that are a mixture of the Eastern wild turkey and the Osceola wild turkey with some colorations in between both. Occur in the panhandle of Florida, the southern tips of Mississippi, Alabama and much of southern Georgia.

Jake. A one-year-old gobbler.

Kee-kee run. The young gobbler's squeal and call.

Longbeard. A name for a dominant or boss gobbler, usually more than two years old.

Lost call. A call, also known as the assembly call, that's given to try and pull a turkey flock together or to locate a gobbler.

Merriam turkey. (Melegris gallopavo merriami) One of six subspecies of North American wild turkey. Found in the western U.S.

Mexican turkey. (Meleagris gallopavo gallopavo) One of six subspecies of North American wild turkey that was originally located in the central part of Mexico and is the forefather of the domestic turkey.

Mouth yelper. A term referring to the diaphragm call.

Ocellated turkey. (Meleagris ocellata) One of six subspecies of North American turkey. Having some blue coloration, the ocellated turkey is found in the Yucatan of Mexico and nearby central American states, is considered to be by many the loveliest wild turkey.

Osceola turkey. (Meleagris gallopavo osceola) One of six subspecies of North American wild turkey found predominantly in Florida and some parts of Southern Mississippi, Alabama and Georgia. The Osceola turkey is darker over most of his body than the Eastern wild turkey.

Owl hooter. A call that when blown reproduces the sound of the barred owl. Used to locate turkey, which will shock gobble to the call.

Pattern board. A sheet of plywood or metal that catches the shot from a discharged shotgun shell. From the pattern board, the hunter can see density and diameter of the shot. Shooting at a pattern board will tell the hunter how effective his shotgun is at set distances.

Poult. A baby turkey.

Predator. An animal that feeds off other animals. Some of the predators of turkey include wild dogs, bobcats, fox, raccoon, eagles, coyote, wolves, crows, skunks, and snakes.

Purr. A contented sound made by a hen.

Push button call. A simple friction call that requires the hunter to push a peg with his finger to produce hen calls.

Putt. An alarm sound given by a turkey that usually indicates danger.

Rio Grande turkey. (Meleagris gallopavo intermedia). A turkey in the western U.S. Usually is larger in weight than most other North American turkey.

Roost. A particular tree where a turkey perches during the night for sleeping.

Scouting. Looking for turkey signs, listening for turkey sounds and becoming aware of the terrain and the habitat so that this information can help in determining a hunt plan.

Set-up. Taking a stand in an area where you determine a turkey should come. A good set-up should be in clean woods with no natural barriers that the turkey will have to cross to get to the hunter.

Shock gobble. The instinctive reaction of a wild turkey in response to some type of loud sound, not necessarily to hen calls. May include the slamming of a car door, the whistling of a train, the clapping of thunder and the calling of a crow.

Slate call. A call that uses a peg that is stroked across a piece of slate to produce the sound and call of the wild turkey.

Snood (snoot). A bump on the forehead of a turkey that changes size according to level of excitement.

Spur. A horny growth on a gobbler's leg. Can occur sometimes in hens. Similar to human fingernails. Multiple spurs may be found, but some gobblers have no spurs. Most gobblers average one-inch spurs at two years.

Striker box. Either a slate-covered or an aluminum-covered wooden box that is used by rubbing a wooden peg across the box to imitate the call of a wild turkey. Also known as a friction call.

Strutting. When a turkey coils his neck, causes his feathers to stand up, spreads his tail and drops his wings to try and impress a hen.

Strut zone. An area where a turkey goes to on a regular basis to strut and hopefully meet a hen for breeding.

Sub-dominant gobblers and hens. Birds in the social order of a turkey flock that are below the longbeard and boss hen.

Tree call/tree yelp. A very soft series of yelps given while the hen turkey is still in the tree before she flies down to the ground. The tree yelp is best described as a quiet yawn.

Tube call. Made of plastic and resembling a miniature megaphone, the tube call has a piece of latex rubber over its end that is blown against by the hunter to make the sounds of the wild turkey.

Wattles. The fatty tissue that looks like globs of skin and fat around a turkey's neck.

Wing-bone call. A call made from a turkey's wing bone. The hunter sucks air through the bone to call. There are also man-made wing-bone calls that resemble pipes.

Yelp. A turkey's call that is a general call that changes in rhythm from turkey to turkey. Can be either a contented or excited yelp.

Index